THE PUB LOV

LONDON

For Sarah, Harrison and Bridie

All photographs Callum Moy

THE PUB LOVER'S GUIDE TO
LONDON
CALLUM MOY

WHITE OWL

AN IMPRINT OF PEN & SWORD BOOKS LTD.
YORKSHIRE – PHILADELPHIA

First published in Great Britain in 2024 by
White Owl
An imprint of
Pen & Sword Books Ltd.
Yorkshire - Philadelphia

ISBN 978 1 39903 552 1

The right of Callum Moy to be identified as author of this work
has been asserted by him in accordance with the Copyright,
Designs and Patents Act 1988.

A CIP catalogue record for this book is available from the
British Library.

Printed and bound in India by Parksons Graphics Pvt. Ltd.
Design: SJmagic DESIGN SERVICES, India.

Pen & Sword Books Ltd. incorporates the imprints of Pen &
Sword Books: After the Battle, Archaeology, Atlas, Aviation,
Battleground, Discovery, Family History, History, Maritime,
Military, Politics, Select, Transport, True Crime, Fiction, Frontline
Books, Leo Cooper, Praetorian Press, Seaforth Publishing,
Wharncliffe and White Owl.

For a complete list of Pen & Sword titles please contact

PEN & SWORD BOOKS LIMITED
George House, Beevor Street, Off Pontefract Road, Hoyle Mill,
Barnsley, South Yorkshire, England, S71 1HN.
E-mail: enquiries@pen-and-sword.co.uk
Website: www.pen-and-sword.co.uk

or

PEN AND SWORD BOOKS
1950 Lawrence Rd, Havertown, PA 19083, USA
E-mail: uspen-and-sword@casematepublishers.com
Website: www.penandswordbooks.com

CONTENTS

1

INTRODUCTION

Pubs and the metropolis

Metropolitan London has around 7,000 public houses – an average of 25 pubs per square mile. No other capital city in the world matches this density. It's not surprising that the London pub is such an institution at home and abroad!

Pubs take their name from being private houses licensed to sell beer to the public. Licensing them was a job creation scheme introduced when unemployment was high after victory in the Napoleonic Wars and the troops demobbed. The Beerhouse Act 1830 was introduced by the Prime Minister of the day, and victor at the Battle of Waterloo, the Duke of Wellington. It permitted anyone to apply for a licence to brew and sell beer from their home – from a public order perspective, it wasn't an entirely satisfactory situation!

Alcohol consumption has been around long before 1830. From the Georgian period (i.e., 1714–1830) its basic form was an alehouse selling only beer. An upgrade was the tavern, having a wider range of drinks such as wine, and a meal. And a coaching inn (see page 7) was a popular station to rest, feed and water horses during a long journey.

The Glorious Revolution in 1688 (see page 54) introduced gin from Holland – the favourite tipple of the new Dutch King William III of England. War with France had restricted the supply of wine and, in any case, its consumption was seen as unpatriotic. With gin, alcohol acquired its negative reputation – as compared to good old 'healthy' beer, immortalised by Hogarth's satirical prints: 'Gin Lane' and 'Beer Street'. Port was also introduced around this time by Portuguese allies in Lisbon.

Pubs were part and parcel of the expansion of London (see chapter 9) – the population of London grew to six million in 1900 (from only one million a hundred years earlier). Acting as accommodation for the navvies and construction workers, pubs were often the first building in a development – accounting for why so many are located on corners, being an edge of the plot.

Because pubs are ubiquitous in the capital, a pub can always be found near a place of historical significance. This book selects some key moments in the history of London, from Roman times to the modern day, and suggests a popular pub nearby to savour the moment – reliving the history with a drink in hand! It is hoped the reader will visit many of the locations and in so doing experience not only some of London's best pubs, but also see where the principal historical events took place.

2

CONQUEST

The Grapes

14 Lime Street, London EC3M 7AN

Claudius succeeds where Julius failed
Emperor Claudius needed a big hit –
and the invasion of England in AD43
was it. With an overwhelming force
of 40,000 troops and elephants he
achieved what Julius Caesar failed
nearly 100 years earlier. But London
wasn't the goal – there was nothing to
it back then. Colchester was the real
prize, home to the Iceni tribe that had
been running guerrilla attacks into
Gaul, brazenly seizing the people and
assets of the western Roman empire.

The invasion force, under the
command of Platius, set off from
Boulogne and landed at Richborough
in Kent before travelling to Canterbury.
Proceeding along the south bank of
the marshy and tidal River Thames, the
lowest crossing point was in London.
And with the aid of a pontoon bridge
the force crossed the 'Tamesis' where
London Bridge stands today.

Heading up Fish Street Hill, then
along Gracechurch Street and on to
Colchester, the Romans quelled the
Iceni and cut a deal with their leader,
King Prasutagus, to cease hostilities
in exchange for his liberty and
allegiance. A few years later Governor
Scapula captured King Caratacus of the
neighbouring Catuvellauni tribe and
paraded him through the streets of
Rome – at least as an honoured captive.

In AD60 Prasutagus died and
Governor Paulinus reneged on Platius'
deal; subsequent conflict led to the
rape of Prasutagus' daughters and the
flogging of his wife, Boudica. A year later
Boudica wreaked revenge by attacking
Londinium's unprepared Roman forces
and British collaborators. The scorched-
earth attack resulted in 70,000 deaths – a
layer of burned earth remains still exists
seven metres below the City today.

The moderate Classicianus replaced
Paulinus and in time the colony thrived.
Londinium was regarded as the *de facto*
capital of Britain and the biggest Roman
town north of the Alps. It was a strategic
location sited between two low hills;
Cornhill (where St Peter's Church probably
became the first site of Christian worship
in London) and Ludgate Hill (topped by
St Paul's Cathedral) – both separated
by the fresh-water River Walbrook.

Above: *The Grapes.*

Below: *Leadenhall Market.*

St Paul's Cathedral (from Roman Watling Street).

River Thames (looking east).

The Thames enabled passage 80 miles inland to Oxford (to access Cotswold wool) and was opposite the River Rhine in the east – the major river flowing through Europe. London would become a key market, importing all types of Mediterranean produce, whilst exporting mainly tin, wool and grain.

In AD43 the Roman invading force marched a stone's throw past where The Grapes is located today – it's an attractive wood-panelled Victorian pub with copper lights hanging over the bar, selling a range of beers and wines. Located in Leadenhall Market, built on the footprint of the Roman Forum, it's an appropriate venue to muse how the market sellers have been replaced by City workers spilling out of Lloyds of London after hours.

The Anthologist

58 Gresham St, London EC2V 5AY

Everyday life in Londinium

After the shock and calamity of the Boudiccan attack – and the responding annihilation of the Iceni – the Romans got to work building a defendable and sustainable capital. The remains of the Roman forum (market) and basilica (town hall) still lie beneath the Victorian Leadenhall Market on Gracechurch Street. The Roman amphitheatre, discovered as recently as 1988, rests underneath Guildhall Yard with a section of it exposed *in situ* in the Guildhall Art Gallery. A Roman fort and garrison were installed near Noble Street, holding 1,000 troops as a deterrent against any further transgressions by the native Celtic tribes – at least those who had not fled to the west of England or Ireland (territories that held no interest to the Romans). Late in the occupation a wall was constructed around the City – today, most evident at Coppers Place. As well as being defensive, it was probably intended as a border crossing to control passage and enforce taxation. The wealthy would hang out at a bathhouse resembling the Billingsgate Roman Baths (having separate tepidarium, caldarium and frigidarium). Whilst the officer class would worship the cult of the god of Mithras at a temple near Walbrook, now splendidly brought to life in the basement of Bloomberg's European headquarters – including an exhibit of the earliest known inscription of 'Londinium' on a wooden tablet.

At its peak in AD200, Londinium had a population of around 100,000 along with the civil infrastructure of a town council. The main imports were olive oil (from Africa and Iberia), wine (from the Rhineland and Mediterranean) and pottery, lamps and tableware from Italy and Gaul. Tin, being a key compound of bronze was Britain's principal export owing to its relative rarity in continental Europe – and along with wool the most likely reason the Romans stayed. Much was learned about everyday life in Londinium from the artefacts recovered from an archaeological dig at Poultry, now exhibited in the (renamed) London Museum.

Decline started in the late 200s when Roman Britain joined a breakaway Gallic empire (although London was later won back for Rome). Reducing imperial trade and conflict in the east with the Huns and Goths resulted in an evaporation of proper funding for London, causing the garrison to mutiny and invade Gaul and Spain for plunder. The Romano-British citizens also revolted due to high taxes. Even the conversion of Emperor Constantine to Christianity in AD312 did little to change the trajectory of decline. By AD410, migrating tribes were causing such disruption in Europe that Roman Emperor Honorius recalled all troops to Rome – leaving London to the mercy of the invading Saxons. Centrally heated homes would not return to London for 1,400 years!

The Anthologist is situated opposite the Guildhall and site of the former Roman Amphitheatre. It's a modern open-plan bar-deli, also serving breakfasts with a strong appeal.

The Anthologist.

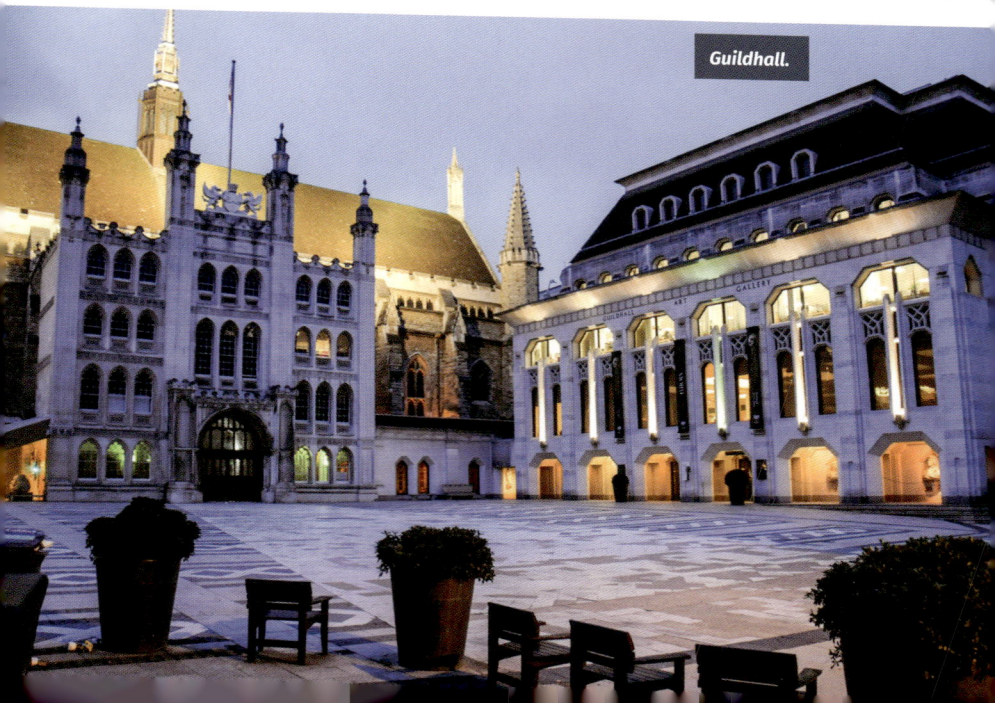

Guildhall.

Williamson's Tavern

1 Groveland Ct, London EC4M 9EH

Barbarians at the gates

With a power vacuum in London (and throughout Britain), the Saxons and their allies, the Angles, had it easy. Without a military force the Romano-British were defenceless and the invaders practically walked in. The Saxons, a semi-nomadic culture, found the Roman stone walls and buildings foreboding and settled outside the City in the area corresponding to Victoria Embankment, Aldwych and Covent Garden today. They called the timber-built settlement Lundenwich and its main thoroughfare, Strand (meaning shoreline).

London belonged to the Kingdom of Essex (the east Saxons). In time the Saxons came to recognise the defensive attraction of the old Roman city and moved within its walls, calling it Lundenberg, and adopting the Roman street patterns. A new port at Queenhithe (near Billingsgate) was established and Aldwych (meaning the old port) was degraded. Cheapside (i.e., 'shop-side') was formed as the main thoroughfare and streets leading off it carried the names of the produce one could purchase (e.g., Bread, Milk, Honey and Fish) and this is still evident today. At the church of All Hallows (by Tower Bridge) we can see the oldest stone arch in London, dated to AD675.

In AD851, the Vikings invaded the Saxon settlement. And despite the city walls, the Saxons succumbed to the ferocity and might of the invaders. Today, St Clement Danes reminds us of the Viking church on the site and the English language is packed with old Norse words (e.g., sky, skin, leg, gun and get). It was over thirty years, in AD886, before the Vikings were repulsed by King Alfred of Wessex and forced to seek terms – leading to a division of the country into southern Saxon and northern Viking-controlled territory. But further incursions continued, some notably stopped by London's Norwegian ally King Olaf II – remembered at locations in Southwark and by the nursery rhyme 'London bridge is falling down', taken as a measure to prevent invasion by the Vikings from the south. Eventually, the Viking Kings Sweyn Forkbeard and Cnut prevailed – becoming Kings of England in 1013 and 1035 respectively.

Cheapside would later become the main route for royal processions between the monarch's palace at the Tower of London and the centre of royal worship at Westminster Abbey.

Situated off Bow Lane on Cheapside, Williamson's Tavern was originally the home of Sir John Fastolf (whose name Shakespeare changed to Falstaff in the *Merry Wives of Windsor*) before becoming a residence for the Lord Mayors of London. The pub dates to the 1600s with twentieth century renovations, although

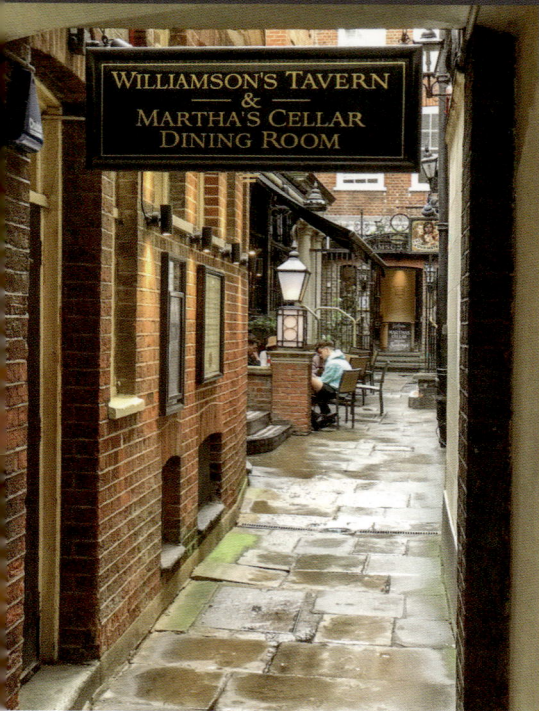

Williamson's Tavern.

St Mary-le-Bow Church, Cheapside.

the fireplace claims to be made of Roman bricks. Inset into the wall of the restaurant there is an inscribed tablet marking the exact centre of the City of London (the 'City').

Hung Drawn and Quartered

26–27 Great Tower St, London EC3R 5AQ

And now the French

William, Duke of Normandy, was aghast at the news that Harold Godwinson had been crowned King Harold II at Westminster Abbey in December 1065. He believed he had been promised succession of the English crown by his pious uncle, King Edward the Confessor, years earlier in Normandy. Edward's passing was followed swiftly by the coronation of Harold II – an act that precipitated a showdown between Harold's and William's forces at the Battle of Hastings. The outcome is well-known. Harold died from arrow in the eye and on Christmas Day 1066

King William I had his coronation at Westminster Abbey. To maintain some form of continuity, William offered an agreement to the civic leaders of London – swear allegiance to me, pay your taxes and I'll leave you alone, to which they conceded. The document charting this agreement, the so-called William Charter, is still cited as the basis of the City of London's independence from the monarchy and HM Government. It can be seen at the Guildhall Art Gallery.

William's builders quickly got to work constructing a series of (Caen) stone castles around the country – the most famous being the Tower of London. Its main fortifications faced north into the City as if in readiness for rebellion. The Tower would become the centre of English monarchy for 500 years, until King Henry VIII moved the royal court to the Palace of Westminster (see page 68). The Tower was variously a palace, a garrison, an armaments store, a prison, a place of execution, a mint, the first location of London Zoo and a place of worship. St John's Chapel is London's oldest. It has hosted many well-known prisoners (e.g., Walter Raleigh, Thomas More and Princess Elizabeth I) and seen some infamous executions (e.g., Anne Boleyn and Catherine Howard).

Hung Drawn and Quartered.

The Normans were the last to conquer England – there would be other attempts (e.g., the Spanish Armanda, the Napoleonic Wars and the Nazis in the Second World War), but none would succeed. The British are now so accustomed to the infiltration of French into the English language that they forget the origins of names such as Bill, Dick and Bob are from the Norman Conquest!

The Hung Drawn and Quartered takes its name from the ghastly death reserved for those convicted of treason. Despite this association, it's ideal to visit before or after a visit to the Tower to sample modern craft beers and cask classics! It is positioned opposite another of London's oldest must-see churches, All Hallows by the Tower, which boasts an original of a Saxon arch, a Roman mosaic pavement and a fascinating 3D model of Roman London.

Did you know? Today, the Tower is best known as the home to the Crown Jewels dating from the Reformation of the monarchy in 1660 – Oliver Cromwell's puritans had the originals melted down to pay for the fledging republic (see page 53).

Tower of London.

The Trafalgar St James

The Rooftop, 2 Spring Gardens, London
SW1A 2TS

Un coup de Trafalgar

Napoleon had assembled a
200,000-strong Grand Armée at
Boulogne and awaited the French fleet
to provide naval cover. His goal was
the invasion of England. In 1805, this
was the most perilous situation facing
England since the Spanish Armanda in
1588. Differences in religion played their
part – but this time it was personal.

Napoleon was intent on eradicating
the British monarchy and installing his
imperial version of republicanism.

Responding to Napoleon's call,
the French fleet sailed north from
the Port of Cadiz. Outside the port
the English fleet, led by Admiral
Lord Horatio Nelson, had laid siege
for weeks, awaiting the moment to
pounce. Deploying some innovative
naval manoeuvres, Nelson outwitted
the French Commander Villeneuve and
after five hours of fighting England
won the day. Invasion was averted, but
tragically at the cost of Nelson's life.

The Trafalgar St James, The Rooftop.

Nelson Column.

He had refused to disguise himself on deck and was picked off by a French sniper. His torn uniform (and the fatal shot) can be seen at the Maritime Museum in Greenwich (see page 42).

Loved by his men, Nelson's loss of an eye and arm in previous conflicts were injuries that proved his mettle – his moderate temper marked him out as a leader beyond many. His men knew he had form with the French, previously defeating French fleets at the Battles of the Nile and Copenhagen.

Trafalgar Square, and its centrepiece the Nelson Column, was completed in 1840. It is London's main square, hosting the National Gallery (see page 121) on its north side and Canadian Embassy on the west – for that most faithful and favoured ally during the American Wars of Independence (see page 73). On the south side of Trafalgar Square is an equestrian statue of King Charles I, dating from 1630 (see pages 41, 53).

The bar at The Rooftop is an excellent venue to view the square and meet Nelson at eye-level, facing out to sea and his beloved fleet. In fine months, you many need to book.

Did you know? Nelson's dying words were probably 'Kismet Hardy', meaning, 'It's my destiny'. Lore goes, that to preserve his body on the return passage to England it was pickled in a barrel of rum, and the cocktail imbibed by his men – giving us the derivation 'to have a stiff drink'!

3

RELIGION

Madison

Rooftop Terrace, One New Change,
London EC4M 9AF

The resurgence of Christianity
That St Paul's was built as a domed
cathedral resembling St Peter's in
Rome, the fountain of Catholicism, is
astonishing. St Paul's Cathedral was
built at the height of conflict between
Protestants and Catholics in London –
ultimately leading to the expulsion of
Catholic-leaning King James II for the
Protestant Dutchman King William III
in the (bloodless) Glorious Revolution
of 1688.

Occupying the small Ludgate Hill, it's
possible the Romans originally built a
wooden temple here in around AD50
to the Goddess Diana. The first century
Roman historian, Tacitus, described
the area as a 'concourse of merchants
and known for the abundance of
its provisions and that the state of
prosperity was due to the noble river
on which it stood; without the Thames,
London could not have existed.'

After the collapse of the western
Roman Empire in the early 500s, and
its retrenchment to the east, Rome
became a city state lead spiritually by
the Pope. In AD597 Pope Gregory the
Great sent a mission, led by Augustine,
to England to reclaim the country for
Christianity. Augustine succeeded in
converting King Ethelred of Kent to
Christianity, probably attracted by the
power that God would confer upon him.
By AD604 the movement had spread to
London and Mellitus was confirmed as
the first Bishop of London. The Bishop
of London still resides at The Deanery
in nearby Dean's Court.

Old St Paul's Cathedral was
destroyed in the Great Fire of London
in 1666 (see page 87). It took over
200 years to complete and incredibly
was larger than today's church – see
the comparative floor plans on the
south exterior of St Paul's. Seven
times a day, monks would walk from
the monastery to the church reciting
the Lord's Prayer – giving rise to the
name of Paternoster (our father)
Square.

A particular tragedy of the Great Fire
is that citizens stored their valuables in
Old St Paul's as protection from the fire.
Being made of stone it was regarded

Madison.

as a haven for valuables, books and documents. But the roof was timber and such was the conflagration that it too caught fire and crashed into the cathedral, creating an inferno.

New St Paul's Cathedral, modelled on St Peter's in Rome, swept away hundreds of years of gothic architecture and introduced the baroque. Its builder, Sir Christopher Wren was a polymath of the time operating simultaneously at the leading-edge of mathematics, astronomy, engineering and the emerging profession of architecture. His partner, Robert Hooke, the quirky engineering genius, devised a method of lightening the structure to prevent it from sinking into the London clay – something one can observe today by visiting the dome and the Golden Gallery, offering spectacular views of London. Such was the expense of the undertaking, that funds were diverted from maintenance work at Westminster Abbey (officially the Collegiate Church of St Peter) to pay for St Paul's – giving rise to the expression 'robbing Peter to pay Paul'.

Today, St Paul's is the resting place of many famous British leaders, most notably Wellington and Nelson who lie side-by-side in the crypt. Wren died in 1723. His modest burial plot in St. Paul's bears a Latin inscription translating to 'Reader, if you seek his memorial, look about you.'

St Paul's Cathedral from New Change.

St Paul's Cathedral from Paternoster Square.

Madison is a vibrant bar and restaurant, very popular with party goers and fashion setters. It is located at the top of New Change, an elevated public space with stunning views of St. Pauls and London. In summer, a wide screen plays Wimbledon. It is a contender for London's best free rooftop space.

The Blackfriar

174 Queen Victoria St, London EC4V 4EG

Monastic life
After the Augustines set up a monastery in Austin Friars, other Catholic Orders from Italy beat a track to England. Benedictine monks established monasteries at St Barts and at Westminster, the Carmelites set up near Fleet Street, the Dominicans at Blackfriars, nuns took up residence at St Helen's Priory and the Franciscans at Greyfriars near St Paul's.

The medieval Blackfriars Dominican monastery was used for great occasions of state, including meetings of Parliament and the Privy Council. King Henry VIII's cardinal, Thomas Wolsey, knew the place well as he attempted to arrange a divorce between the king and his queen Catherine of Aragon – resulting in an inconclusive trial held by Cardinal Wolsey and the Papal Legate in 1529. After he died of a heart attack Wolsey's work was continued by Thomas Cromwell.

Following King Henry VIII's break from Rome in 1534, his officious chancellor (Thomas Cromwell) persuaded him that monasteries were hotbeds of dissent, profligacy and debauchery that needed dissolution. Henry's acquiescence resulted in one of the biggest seizures of land in British history between 1536 and 1541 – and sores that took nearly 500 years to heal between what became the Church of England (under Henry's son) and the Roman Catholic Church. In London, the Carthusian order at Charterhouse held out the longest and suffered the worst for it. The Archbishop of Canterbury and Pope John Paul II finally found peace in each other's company at Canterbury Cathedral in 1982.

During the Dissolution, the many social services provided by monasteries ceased abruptly. Services like education, healthcare, food for the poor, and not least, spiritual guidance. In time, these would be replaced by royal patronage, but it was a long transition. Church land was divided and sold between Henry's favourites and followers. The many ecclesiastical palaces on Strand were acquired by aristocrats, with the remaining land becoming the King's Crown Estate (today still owned by the monarch but managed by the government, with its proceeds going to the state).

The Dissolution provided enormous wealth to the monarchy, much of it invested to build a world-class navy

The Blackfriar.

on the site of the old Dominican friary, the pub's name recalls the black habits worn by the local Dominican monks.

The Westminster Arms

9–10 Storey's Gate, London SW1P 3AT

The west monastery

Fable has it that fisherman saw a vision of St Peter fishing in the Thames by the site of today's Victoria Tower Gardens. Word quickly spread to the Benedictine monks in the City, who promptly moved two miles west to build a small wooden church near the venerated spot, a marshy, overgrow area outside the City. The aptly named Thorney Street provides its western boundary today. In AD960 the Bishop of London, St Dunstan, later provided funds to build a larger wooden church.

King Edward the Confessor (named for his piety) paid for a stone church to be built on the site in 1065 and lived just long enough for Westminster Abbey to be dedicated in December 1065. Westminster was the west monastery – in contrast to St Paul's in the east. King William I, realising the significance of the Abbey, had himself crowned here on Christmas Day in 1066 seated in the same coronation chair. Westminster Abbey (or more fully, the Collegiate Church of St Peter, Westminster) is the personal property of the monarch. Termed a 'Royal Peculiar' it is under the jurisdiction of a Dean and Chapter,

capable of protecting the islands from the superpowers of the day, Spain and France. Without the sale of Catholic church land, it's unlikely Britain would have evolved into the superpower it became in the eighteenth century.

Saved by a campaign led by the late poet laureate Sir John Betjeman, the Art Nouveau interior of the Blackfriar pub displays copper reliefs of jolly monks at work by artist Henry Poole and sculptor Frederick Callcott – extolling their commitment to the free-thinking Arts and Crafts movement. Being situated subject only to the monarch and not the Church of England.

In 1245, King Henry III expanded the Abbey, positioning the tomb of King Edward the Confessor at its centre. It is largely King Henry's abbey that we see today, with the addition of the west-facing towers in 1745. It was a fully functionary monastic abbey and was left untouched by Henry VIII at the Dissolution. Dean's Yard is free to access, despite the guarded barrier, and provides some pleasant green space plus magnificent views of the Abbey. Also in Dean's Yard is Westminster School, originally founded by the Benedictine monks.

The school's survival was confirmed by royal patronage of Queen Elizabeth I in 1560. It's a delight to watch the pupils play football in the yard amidst all this splendour and tradition.

All royal coronations (except for Edwards V and VIII) have taken place in the Abbey, following the solemn tradition of the oath of allegiance, anointing with holy oil, investiture and regalia – seated on the thirteenth century coronation chair placed on the mosaic 'Cosmati' pavement. The founder of the Tudor dynasty, Henry VII, is buried with his queen Elisabeth of York in the 'Lady Chapel', an extension to the Abbey built in 1540. In a nearby chapel his

The Westminster Arms.

Westminster Abbey.

Walls of the original Palace of Westminster.

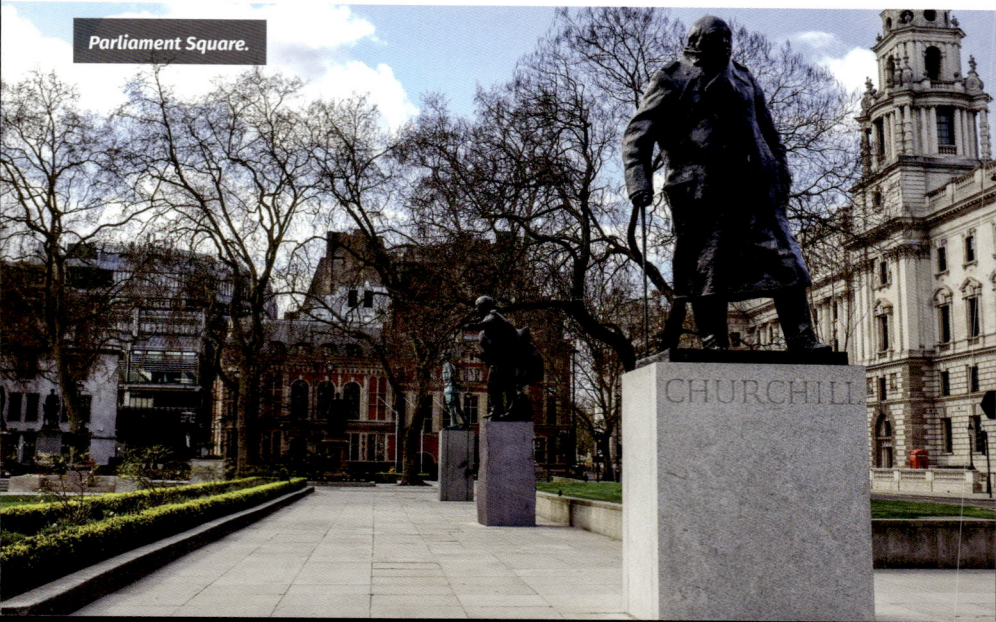

Parliament Square.

The Prince and Princess of Wales leaving Westminster Abbey on their wedding day.

granddaughter, Queen Elizabeth I, and Mary I share the touching epitaph 'Partners both in throne and grave, here rest we two sisters, Elizabeth and Mary, in the hope of one resurrection.' Poets' Corner is the resting place of many from the arts, including Geoffrey Chaucer, Charles Dickens, Alfred Tennyson and George Fredrick Handel, whilst the sciences are represented by Isaac Newton, Charles Darwin and, more recently, Stephen Hawking – just a selection of around 3,000 burials in the Abbey.

The Westminster Arms is situated nearby, in the heart of constitutional monarchical London. It's also a favourite with Members of Parliament who on hearing the division bell installed in the pub, can dash back to the Houses of Parliament to vote.

The Hand & Shears

1 Middle St, Barbican, London EC1A 7JA

Not such a smooth field

Whilst on a pilgrimage to Rome in the twelfth century, Rahere, a religious courtier to King Henry I, came down with malaria. Clinging to life he promised that upon recovery he would build a hospital for the sick in London. Recovered and travelling home he had vision of St Bartholomew – and true to his word Rahere founded a priory and hospital in his name. The church of St Bartholomew the Great, its priory and hospital, have provided continuous spiritual and medical care in Smithfield from 1123 to the present day – the longest period of any hospital (on the same site) in England. A Medical School was formally recognised in 1822 and a School of Nursing in 1877 (following the example set by the Nightingale School at St Thomas' Hospital).

Being an open expanse, Smithfield (derived from 'smooth field') was favoured for tournaments and later executions – notably that of the Scottish patriot Sir William Wallace (the bane of King Edward I) in 1305. Smithfield also saw an assembly of the forces in the Peasants Revolt, spawned by the Poll Tax of 1381. Abruptly ending, in the presence of the boy-king Richard II, with the revolt's leader Wat Tyler being slain by Sir William Walworth, Mayor of London. Smithfield would become London's 'execution-central' until replaced by Tyburn (at Hyde Park Corner) in the eighteenth century and Newgate in the nineteenth century (see page 81). During the reign of Queen Mary I, Protestant heretics were

The Hand & Shears.

routinely burned at Smithfield (to purify their souls) – matched later by burnings of Catholics at Tyburn during the reign of Queen Elizabeth I.

Rahere started a tradition of healthcare for which London would become world-renowned. St Thomas' Hospital in Southwark (named after Thomas Becket) was next in 1173 – the bespoke 'Old Operating Theatre' was added in 1820 and remains a fascinating visitor attraction today. Military hospitals were established for the army in Chelsea (Royal Hospital Chelsea, 1682) and the navy in Greenwich (Royal Naval Hospital, 1694). An expansion of hospitals in the Georgian period followed with Westminster (1719), Guys (1725), St George's (1733), London (1740) and Middlesex (1745) – many still operating today. In 1741, Thomas Coram established the Foundling Hospital for abandoned babies (the museum of the same name can be visited today).

St Bartholomew's Priory held an annual 'Cloth Fair', later becoming the popular Bartholomew Fair (see London's oldest house at 41 Cloth Fair). The fair encouraged a permanent market, regarded by Daniel Defoe in 1726 as the greatest in the world. And by 1850, livestock would be 'violently forced into London' leading to diabolical conditions and a threat to human health. By this time the ancient fair had also become renowned for debauched and offensive behaviour.

The sheep and cattle market along with the fair closed in 1856. Meat is still traded at the modern Smithfield Market, supplying inner city butchers, shops and restaurants, and fittingly the London Museum is now housed in the old General and Fish Market building.

The Hand and Shears, a favourite of workers from the Smithfield Meat Market and nurses from St Barts Hospital, is well-known for its real ales and craft beers as well as seasonal local beers and ciders.

While in the area, also try to find Ye Olde Mitre, Holborn (at 1 Ely Court,

Ye Olde Mitre.

41 Cloth Fair.

Ely Place) – which takes the undisputed title of London's toughest pub to find! Established in 1546, its clientele may have included Elizabeth I, given she granted the surrounding land to her favourite, Sir Christopher Hatton, in the 1560s – although the current building dates from around 1772. It is technically still part of the Diocese of Ely, Cambridgeshire, a quirk due to it originally being a meeting place for the servants of the nearby Palace of the Bishops of Ely.

The Edgar Wallace

40 Essex St, Temple, London WC2R 3JE

Law will prevail

The Knights Templar were an order of crusading monks founded in the early twelfth century who followed the classic monastic vows of poverty and chastity, but also vowed to protect pilgrims on their way to the Holy Land. London, having many orders of monks who encouraged pilgrimages east, needed their services. The Knights Templar settled in the area known as Temple today, where they founded a church, just south of Fleet Street, which can still be visited.

Temple Church (so named because the knights' church in Jerusalem was located where the ancient of Temple of Solomon once stood), is one of London's oldest churches. Of its two parts, the round church (modelled on the Church of the Holy Sepulchre in Jerusalem) was consecrated in 1185 whilst the chancel was added in 1240. Most of the original structure survives today, with some Wren refurbishments, nineteenth century 'beautifications' and major repairs after the Blitz. Like Westminster Abbey, it is a Royal Peculiar coming under the direct jurisdiction of His Majesty. William Marshal (the 'greatest knight that ever lived'), champion of King Henry II and guardian to the young King Henry III, is buried here, along with his sons.

Upon the suppression of the Knights Templar (and the subsequent Knights Hospitallers) at the Dissolution, the land and property passed to the Crown. Later in 1609, King James I granted ownership of the area to lawyers (who had been leasing the land) on the proviso they maintained the Temple Church. Today, the legal Inns of Inner Temple and Middle Temple still maintain the church – the Inner Temple goes by the sign of a Pegasus whilst Middle Temple is represented by the Lamb and Flag. At Temple, there is a plethora of historical buildings, fountains and gardens all open to the public in this truly secret part of London. The rollcall of famous associations is endless (e.g., Walter Raleigh, John Evelyn, Edmund Burke and Charles Dickens). Like Queen Elizabeth I, you can even lunch in the Great Hall built in 1573. Surviving the Blitz, it was also earlier famously home to the first performance of Shakespeare's *Twelfth Night*, in 1601.

The Edgar Wallace pub, named after a prominent fleet Street journalist, is a favourite of lawyers from both the legal Inns, with few tourists or onlookers. The ceiling is packed with the landlord's quirky collection of beer mats and motifs – resembling a museum of advertising for beers, sherry, port and tobacco – the exclusion of music and laptops furthers its appeal to a bygone era.

The Edgar Wallace.

The Mayflower

117 Rotherhithe St, London SE16 4NF

On a prosperous wind

In 1620, the *Mayflower* started its journey to the New World. The *Mayflower* left Rotherhithe under the command of Captain Christopher Jones with around 30 passengers. It sailed to Southampton for supplies and more passengers, also picking up leading puritan and future governor of Plymouth Colony, William Bradford. On 6 September 1620, Jones with 102 passengers and 30 crew members finally set sail across the Atlantic Ocean – on 'a prosperous wind' in the words of Bradford. All were intent on escaping Anglican England – and the concept that the monarch could be head of the church. After nearly two months, land was first sighted off Cape Cod and strong winter seas forced anchorage at Plymouth Rock – further north than the intended destination of more temperate Virginia. The Pilgrim Fathers had arrived in America, establishing Plymouth Colony.

Whilst here, do visit the nearby Brunel Museum in Railway Avenue – showcasing the shaft of the first tunnel known to have been constructed successfully underneath a navigable river. Built by Marc Brunel it connects Rotherhithe with Wapping and is still in use by trains today. Descend the Victorian spiral iron staircase and marvel at this engineering feat of 1843, described as the Eighth Wonder of the World when it opened. Today, near the tunnel at Rotherhithe is a commemorative plaque erected by the American Civil Engineers and the British Institution of Civil Engineers – it celebrates Brunel's tunnel as one of the most important civil engineering sites in the world.

The Mayflower pub in Rotherhithe village is near the spot (30 metres downstream where a plaque marks the exact place) that the Pilgrim Fathers berthed the *Mayflower*, before setting sail in 1620. Originally built in 1550 and called The Shippe Inn, then the Spread Eagle, the pub was renamed The Mayflower in 1956. In this smart and historic place, sign the 'descendants book', leaving your permanent mark in history. It is also the only pub licensed to sell US postage stamps!

Did you know? It's well known that the life of Captain John Smith (leader of the fledgling colony) was saved by the Native American, Pocahontas – but it's less well known that she married the tobacco planter John Rolfe. As Rebecca Rolfe, she chose to return to England where, fêted, she became central to raising 'inward investment' for Jamestown! Pocahontas died at Gravesend (at the age of 21) and is buried at the local Church of St George. The new Virginia Quay monument was completed in 1999, comprising a bronze plaque and stonework from former memorials.

The Mayflower.

Memorial to Captain Christopher Jones, Rotherhithe.

Jamestown, Virginia as the first (permanent) English colony in North America. Despite challenging conditions and a dwindling population, tobacco plants (from seeds in North Carolina) thrived. More settlers arrived and a tobacco-based colony was established. Astonishingly, British exports of tobacco, sugar and fish from its American colonies would soon outstrip England's traditional exports of wool and tin.

Gordon's Wine Bar

47 Villiers St, London WC2N 6NE

A Palace for Uncle Peter

Strand evolved from the Saxon period as the main ecclesiastical highway between the king (living at the Tower of London) and his church (at Westminster Abbey). It was therefore a desirable place for Bishops and aristocracy to establish a London residence and prove allegiance to the crown. Savoy Place was one of the most magnificent, being the residence of Peter II of Savoy, uncle to Queen Eleanor of Provence, wife of King Henry III. It later became a residence of the Dukes of Lancaster before being destroyed in the Peasants Revolt of 1381 – all that remains is the Savoy Chapel, a church still belonging to the current Duke of Lancaster, i.e., King Charles III. After iterations of different buildings throughout the early modern period the site became the

Traveller's tip: If the early days of emigration to America interests you, further downstream is a monument to the embarkation point of the earlier Virginia Quay settlers, under Captains Christopher Newport and John Smith. There were three ships in the flotilla: the *Susan Constant*, the *Godspeed* and the *Discovery*. Arriving in America in 1607, the puritan settlers established

Gordon's Wine Bar.

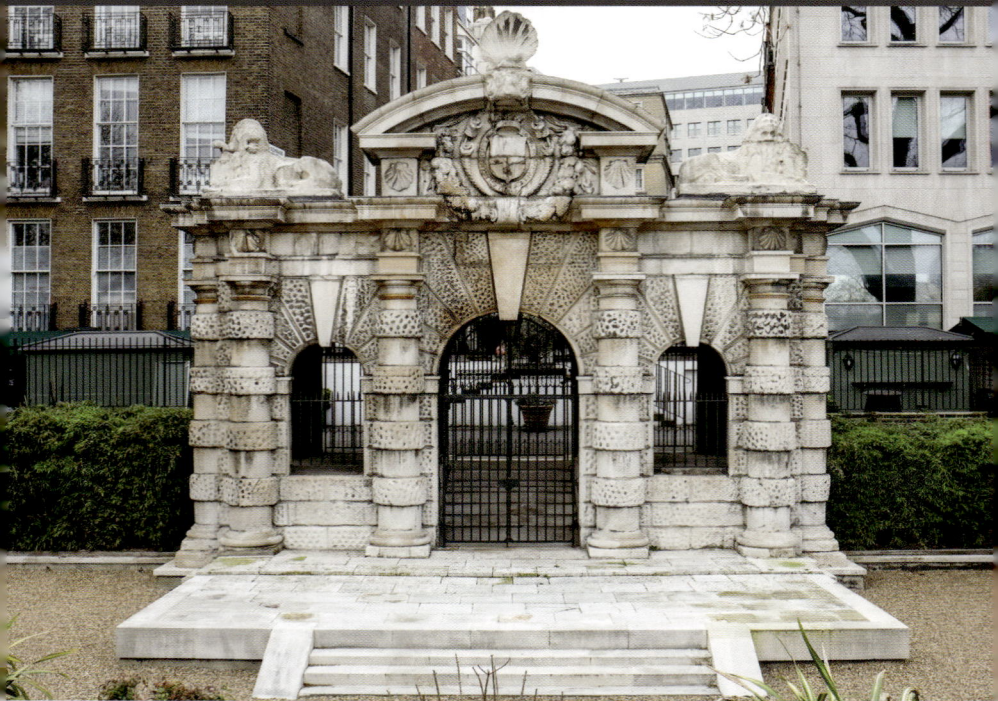

York Watergate.

home of the Savoy Theatre and Savoy Hotel.

Strand was also home to the Bishops of Durham and York, the Dukes of Somerset (Lord Protector during the minority of the future King Edward VI in 1547) and Norfolk (the Howards, whose seat is Arundel Castle), the Earl of Essex (Robert Deveraux, stepson of Queen Elizabeth I's ardent suitor Robert Dudley). These names are all evident today in the streets and building names on Strand.

Somerset House has an illustrious past. Once the home of queens of the realm before becoming the first home of the Royal Academy of Arts and then a government tax office. Today it is an exhibition, retail and restaurant complex occupying a grand neoclassical building that you may recognise from films such as *The Duchess* and *Tomorrow Never Dies.*

The Savoy Theatre was established in 1889 by the impresario Richard D'Oyly Carte as a place to perform works in partnership with writers W.S. Gilbert and Arthur Sullivan. The men produced many operas, the most successful being *The Mikado* and *The Pirates of Penzance* and *Patience*. It was the first public building in the world to be lit entirely by electricity – enabling, for the first time, audiences to properly see the faces of the actors' and admire the scenery. Such was the success of the theatre that the Savoy Hotel was built – still one of London's most luxurious hotels and home to the American Bar, the original and best place for a cocktail. It is where Cesar Ritz started his career, before establishing his own chain of hotels.

At the bottom of Villiers Street, York Watergate is all that remains of York House. Originally built by the Bishop of Norwich in the middle ages, York House came into the possession of Queen Mary I who presented it to the Archbishop of York in 1556, when it acquired its name. (She donated it as compensation for losing York Place in Whitehall to her father King Henry VIII during the Reformation.) In the 1620s, it was purchased by George Villiers, the 1st Duke of Buckingham and favourite of King James I and his son King Charles I. Villiers' prominence eventually resulted in his assassination by jealous officials. His son, the 2nd Duke, married the daughter of General Fairfax (Commander-in-Chief of the New Model Army, see page 53). Having no heir, he sold York House to developers in 1672 with the proviso that all the surrounding streets should remember his name and full title – look out for George Street, Villiers Street, Duke Street, Buckingham Street and even 'Of' Alley!

Established in 1890, Gordon's Wine Bar is one of London's oldest wine bars and its most atmospheric – being based in underground cellars used as air raid shelters in the Second World War on the former site of York House. A candlelight experience that will sear itself into your memory over some beer, wine and traditional British dishes.

4

ROYALTY

The Trafalgar Tavern

Park Row, London SE10 9NW

A dynasty is born

During the fifteenth century, London's merchants and elite supported the Yorkists in the infamous Wars of the Roses. So, in 1485, somewhat 'cap in hand' they greeted the victor of the Battle of Bosworth Field, the Lancastrian Henry Tudor – soon to become King Henry VII. Henry settled in Greenwich and embellished an existing manor house to create the Palace of Placentia – the future place of birth of Henry VIII, Mary I and Elizabeth I.

The palace has gone, but on its site Wren designed the Royal Naval Hospital, Greenwich (at the instruction of Queen Mary II) opening in 1694 to house injured and aged sailors. The hospital remained for nearly 200 years, until becoming the Royal Naval College in 1873 and then from 1998 Greenwich University. You may recognise its buildings from many films, most notably Les Misérables in 2012. Highlights include Thornhill's Baroque Painted Hall (that hosted the lying-in-state of Lord Nelson in 1806) and the National Maritime Museum – an exposition of Britain's seafaring past.

Greenwich is steeped in history. On the hill overlooking the Thames is the Royal Observatory, sponsored by King Charles II, and the Meridian Line – the Prime Meridian of the world designated to be zero longitude. The Queen's House (completed in 1636) is the first truly classical building in England. With its uninterrupted views of the river, Inigo Jones worked on the project for over 20 years, first for James I and then his son Charles I – each gifting the house to their queens.

Near Greenwich Market (an eclectic open-air market) the record-breaking 1869 tea clipper *Cutty Sark* can be visited in dry dock. Famed for its speed that enabled traders to secure top prices in London for the first crop of tea from China, or wool from Australia, it was state-of-the art engineering that enjoyed a glittering career, before its sleek lines were made redundant by the opening of the Suez Canal and the arrival of steam-powered ships.

The Trafalgar Tavern has an enviable riverside location, to the east of the

Trafalgar Tavern.

Cutty Sark.

busy throng of visitors that descend on Greenwich for many weekends of the year. Plentiful internal and outside space ensures seating after visiting the spectacles of maritime Greenwich. Separate dining rooms are adorned with artefacts and paintings telling the story of Britain's great naval history – allowing one to contemplate the royal connections, naval importance and trading wealth brought to London via Greenwich.

Right: *Chapel of St Peter and St Paul, Greenwich.*

Below: *Queen's House, Greenwich.*

The Clarence

53 Whitehall, London SW1A 2HP

Centre of the Royal Court

Henry VIII eyed the resplendent and extensive grounds of York Place, across the river from his temporary residence of Lambeth Palace, at the pleasure of the Archbishop of Canterbury. His own residence, Westminster Palace, had suffered a ruinous fire in 1512 and York Place was now his target. York Place was the London residence of the Archbishop of York, Cardinal Wolsey and through coercion Henry acquired it, forcing the archbishop to remove to his country residence – Hampton Court Palace (that Henry also acquired later in life!). Henry renamed York Place the Palace of Whitehall and granted Westminster 'city' status. Whitehall continued as the principal residence of English monarchs until 1698, when it burned down leaving only the stone-built Banqueting House – one of London's finest visitor attractions today.

James I adorned Banqueting House with baroque ceiling paintings by the Dutchman Peter Paul Rubens, glorifying the union of the English and Scottish crowns (James I was the first joint monarch in 1603) and the

The Clarence.

Banqueting House.

apotheosis of James I. Both James, and his son Charles I, adhered to the divine right of kings. In a tragic turn of fate for Charles I he would step out of the first-floor window of Banqueting House onto the scaffold for his 'second wedding day' with Christ the Lord at his execution in 1649 (see page 54).

Whitehall is a masterclass of classical architecture, resembling the Palazzos of many Italian cities, showcasing the work of, among others, Inigo Jones and George Gilbert-Scott – bucking the trend for English (Christian) Gothic Revival popular for churches and government buildings from 1840 (e.g., the Houses of Parliament, see page 68). Further north on Whitehall is The Admiralty (or Ripley Building), location of British naval commanders and planners for 200 years, and the War Office (connecting to the nearby Churchill War Rooms).

The Clarence is an upmarket pub opposite The Admiralty. It has a good range of Young's beers and wines and specialises in many varieties of gin. The grand first floor dining room features a ceiling frieze of the world map with a nautical theme – reflecting its position as the Admiralty's local.

Above: *The Admiralty.*

Left: *Horse Guards Parade (commemorating Charles I).*

Above: *Lambeth Palace.*

Right: *Sentry Box, Horse Guards.*

BEWARE
HORSES MAY KICK
OR BITE!
THANK YOU

The Red Lion

23 Crown Passage, London SW1Y 6PP

The Court of St James's

When Henry VIII acquired York Place, he also purchased 20 acres of land to its west (from a Christian mission to St James for lepers) and created a private royal hunting park. Here, Henry built a lodge to meet with his favourites and have trysts with admirers. Today, St James's Park is London's oldest park and a haven of extensive breeds of wildfowl – along with tame squirrels and parakeets! The lodge has grown into St James's Palace, and today is the 'Royal Court of the Monarch of the United Kingdom'. It has seen numerous royal births (Queen Anne losing 17 children at birth or infancy) and christenings – plus hosting Charles I's last night before his execution. Today, it is the residence of the Prince of Wales.

St James's Park was enhanced with an 800m-long canal by King Charles II (possibly copying the canal at Versailles that he became familiar with during exile in France) and later received an extensive 'romantic' makeover in 1820 by John Nash, the famous Regency architect. The park and lake are at the southern end of a sweep of development built under the patronage of the Prince Regent (future King George IV), stretching north up Regent Street to The Regent's Park.

On the west side of Whitehall is Horse Guards Parade, the ceremonial parade ground and scene of Trooping the Colour on the monarch's official birthday in June. Most days, at 11am (Sunday 10am) and 4pm, one can see the Changing of the King's Life Guard – a horse-mounted version of the daily ceremony at Buckingham Palace (see below).

At the western end of St James's Park, the white Portland stone of Buckingham Palace fronts the yellow Bath stone of the original palace to its rear. Queen Victoria instructed the Portland stone extension to accommodate her large family, and in the development also relocated the triumphal Marble Arch (that stood at the front of the palace) to the top of Park Lane. Before Queen Victoria chose to live at Buckingham Palace it was known as The Queen's House – having originally been purchased by King George III for his Queen Charlotte in 1762. Most days, at 11am, the Changing of the Guard takes place at Buckingham Palace – rotating between the five regiments of the King's Foot Guard, recognised by the colour of their plumes – Irish (blue), Welsh (green/ white), Grenadiers (white), Coldstream (red) and Scots (none).

The dimly lit Red Lion (one of many in London named after the Scottish King James I) is a 400-year-old pub, purported to have the second oldest beer licence in the West End. Its

The Red Lion.

Regent Street.

Regent Canal.

proximity to St James's Palace qualifies it as the monarch's local – and was secretly patronised by Charles II and Nell Gwynn, who lived in nearby Pall Mall. To this day, it's still regarded as a Royalist pub – visit after the annual procession in January (that commemorates the death of Charles I) and you'll rub shoulders with cavaliers in full dress. Its location in the tunnel-like Crown Passage adds to its appeal.

The Ship Tavern

12 Gate St, London WC2A 3HP

Killing a king

Ruling by divine right, Charles I did not take kindly to parliamentary democracy. Long before the concept of public services and income tax (introduced in 1799), he ruled through his Privy Council raising funds by passing arbitrary royal taxes and authorising trade outside the established system of livery companies. When more significant funds were required (e.g., for warfare) Charles would call a parliament. His arbitrary taxes angered parliamentarians and City traders and furthermore it was suspected he wished to reintroduce Catholicism as the national religion. Charles' appointment of William Laud (who favoured Catholic doctrines) as the Archbishop of London, and later the as the Archbishop of Canterbury along

with a new Common Prayer Book (that adopted Catholic liturgy) fuelled the discontent.

Charles viewed a core group of parliamentarians as mainly responsible for stoking resentment towards him. In 1642, he stormed parliament with armed troops seeking their capture – but the 'birds had flown' and taken refuge in the Guildhall. After failing to enter Guildhall, and with a failed military coup added to his list of transgressions and violations, Charles fled to Nottingham and raised the Royal Standard. Battle lines were drawn between the Cavaliers (royalists) and the Roundheads (parliamentarians) throughout the country.

London was a parliamentarian stronghold, but much of the army sided with the royalists. Oliver Cromwell and General Fairfax set about recruiting a disciplined New Model Army and fortifying the capital with a ring of earth walls and forts. The army trained in Lincoln's Inn Fields, London's largest city square. For seven years the ensuing civil war and Charles's political double-dealings tore the country apart and eliminated any possibility of the monarch's return to rule. A decisive victory was finally had for the parliamentarians at Naseby in 1645, and a year later Charles surrendered to Scottish protection in return for agreeing to Presbyterianism

The Ship Tavern.

Upon the death of Charles I, the monarchy was abolished and the Commonwealth of England was established with Oliver Cromwell as Lord Protector. The so-called Interregnum lasted 11 years until, by a combination of royalist sympathies and a dislike for Puritanism, Charles I's son Charles II was invited to return as monarch in 1660, in what's known as the Restoration of the Monarchy. The 'merry monarch' reinstituted not only royal ceremony, but theatre and Christmas and promised concessions for non-Anglicans and religious dissenters. For 25 years Charles II led peacefully, managing the crises of the Great Plague (1665) and the Great Fire (1666) that beset London.

Upon Charles' death in 1685, and having sired no legitimate children, he was succeeded by his Catholic younger brother, James II. But again, it was widely suspected that James' objective was to reintroduce Catholicism as the official church and rule as an absolutist monarch like his father, Charles I. In response, the king's leading opponents invited the Dutch Prince William of Orange to become the monarch of England. William accepted and a vast invasion force landed peacefully in Devon on 5 November 1688. The Glorious Revolution led to a constitutional monarchy restricted by laws such as the Bill of Rights (1689) and the Act of Settlement (1701). (Limits on the power of the monarch were

in Scotland – a deal subsequently matched by Parliamentarians along with a large cash sum. The Scots handed Charles over and he found himself under house arrest at Hampton Court Palace. After further machinations and escapades, the king was put on trial in Westminster Hall. Found guilty of high treason against the realm of England and sentenced to execution his final words on 30 January 1649 were, 'I go from a corruptible to an incorruptible Crown, where no disturbance can be.'

Lincoln's Inn Fields.

originally agreed in the Magna Carta (1215) but had been marginalised by Charles I.)

There has been a pub on the site of the Ship Tavern since 1549. It's likely the pub was first constructed to satiate the thirst of farm labourers. At the English Reformation, the pub was a haven for Catholic priests and held secret Catholic services. In the 1650s it was popular with parliamentary soldiers training in nearby Lincoln's Inn Fields. Traditional English real-ales served within mahogany-panelled walls and an upstairs dining room lend to its historic pedigree.

5

INDUSTRY AND COMMERCE

Old Dr Butler's Head

2 Mason's Avenue, London EC2V 5BT

The wheels of commerce

The City of London, the 'Square Mile', is world-renowned as a centre of global commerce and finance – if it were an independent country it would rank in the world's top ten measured by GDP. This position of pre-eminence has been achieved by promoting entrepreneurship, fostering free trade and protecting global trade routes – all borne out of the early days of City livery companies.

In the middle ages, in common with many European cities, London had developed a system of trade associations that controlled, for each commodity, who was authorised to trade. On qualifying as a member of the association and upon payment of a fee (a guild), representatives were entitled to wear a uniform that identified them as authorised purveyors complying to quality and price standards. These trade associations became known as livery companies – the first in London was the Weavers established in 1135. Over time, they were joined by around 100 more; the most important were called 'The Great Twelve' – with Mercers (silks and general merchandise), Grocers (spices and measures) and Drapers topping the table. Livery companies operated other forms of governance (e.g., discipline of members, social and health care and education). Recognising this, they combined to create new City-wide functions (e.g., planning, defence and hygiene) and a democratically elected local government – headquartered at Guildhall and led by a Lord Mayor residing at the Mansion House. These historic buildings can be visited today.

This system of local government was established hundreds of years before the English Parliament (see page 68) and still operates today in the City of London. Any member of the public can join the monthly Court of the Common Council to observe the proceedings. The City of London Council is like other municipal authorities, but with some special privileges founded in the William Charter of 1067. These permit a level of autonomy and independence from the monarch's parliament (e.g., method of election to the Common Council, permission to retain cash surplus and a permanent representative based in the UK Parliament: 'The Remembrancer'). Today, the livery companies are charitable bodies donating millions of pounds to good causes, drawing revenue from large land banks in prime locations of the City.

The Guildhall, and its adjoining art gallery, is based in Guildhall Yard. Over the years, it has suffered damage caused by the Great Fire and enemy bombing in the Second World War. However, the walls of the gothic building date from 1428 – qualifying it as the oldest secular building in London. It's not unsurprising the Guildhall is located directly above the Roman Amphitheatre (see page 13), whose stone was repurposed for Saxon civic buildings in later centuries. But City archaeologists only discovered the Amphitheatre in 1988, right underneath their noses in Guildhall Yard!

The nearby Mason's Avenue is home to The Old Doctor Butler's Head. It is one of London's most atmospheric pedestrian-only streets resembling a Tudor alleyway.

The Old Doctor Butler's Head.

Above: *Grocers' Livery Company.*

Below: *Banner of the Mercers' Livery Company.*

Fishmongers' Livery Company.

The pub dates from the late seventeenth century and takes its name from a 'miracle cure' doctor, who specialised in medicinal ales – hence the association! Today, the pub serves a range of (non-medicinal) ales and food. In summer patrons spill into the avenue, making it a particularly British drinking experience.

The Jamaica Wine House

St Michael's Alley, London EC3V 9DS

The City triumphs

In the sixteenth century, London had no international wholesale market matching the best in Europe, in particular the Antwerp Bourse. In 1571, a prominent City trader named Thomas Gresham put that right, when he and others financed the building of an exchange on a site provided by the Mercers' Livery Company. Queen Elizabeth I opened the building and named it the Royal Exchange – for the trading of goods and alcohol, and the arrangement of credits and loans between merchants. Today, and a couple of major fires later, a grand Victorian restoration stands – true to its heritage as London's most upmarket shopping centre. It is on the steps of the Royal Exchange that Royal Proclamations (e.g., royal deaths and the dissolution of Parliament) are read out by a herald.

Merchants of all commodities traded at the new exchange, except for stockbrokers who dealt in the new trade of shares in joint stock companies – some holding royal charters to adventure to foreign lands in pursuit of rare commodities: animal pelts, spices, nuts, sugar and, dreadfully, people. Since share certificates were not yet considered real assets and stockbrokers were being seen as loud and rude, they were expelled from the exchange. In response, stockbrokers relocated to the newly founded coffee houses in nearby Exchange Alley. Places like Pasqua Rosee, Jonathan's and Garraway's proved so popular that the range of services at these places was extended to include commodity trading, insurance and ship underwriting. The latter concentrating at Edward Lloyd's coffee house where one would agree to insure against loss at sea by writing your name under the name of the vessel (i.e., underwriting). Lloyd's extended services again to include the checking and registration of the seaworthiness of vessels (Lloyd's Insurance and Lloyd's Register started life in a coffee house!).

Jonathan's was first to maintain a list of stock prices and its popularity led to it being called The Stocks Exchange – an institution that survived up to 1986, before the advent of electronic share trading. Newly arrived commodities were checked and auctioned at Garraway's. A pin would be inserted perpendicularly into a candle to

The Jamaica Wine House.

Royal Exchange.

Sky Garden building from Lombard Street.

allow a set time for bargaining – as the wax burned through and silenced descended 'one could hear a pin drop'. At any coffee house a tip could be left 'To Insure Promptness'.

The Jamaica Wine House is a challenge to find. Built on the site of Pasqua Rosee's coffee shop, it is nestled in a warren of alleyways south of the Royal Exchange. The atmosphere in the pub and alleyways outside is best experienced after work, preferably on a Thursday when traders vie for

bragging rights on the business of the day – add breeches, tricorn hats and frock coats and it's a blast from the past. The adjacent George and Vulture restaurant was a favourite of Charles Dickens and offers affordable English fare today.

The Ned

27 Poultry, London EC2R 8AJ

Credit rules the waves

The Bank of England is known today for setting the interest rate and being the 'lender of last resort', should a UK bank default on its depositors and debts. It's a venerable public institution, an imposing building and a fortress for the gold reserves of the UK – stored in vaults 30 metres below ground, some £130 billion of bullion.

It started out as the private bank of the government, issuing shares with guaranteed high dividends to wealthy citizens, secured against government assets. This method of raising government funds was novel for the period, when normally if the government required money it was forced to raise funds via one-off taxation – both finite and unpopular. The idea that the government could manage a national debt was the brainchild of Scotsman William Patterson – and it's a habit that continues to this day!

It was an innovation necessitated by William III's wars with the French – the

The Ned.

Bank of England.

architecture complete with the scandal-causing bare-chested 'Lothbury Ladies' above the front door.

The Ned, named after the acclaimed architect Edwin Lutyens, was the headquarters building of the Midland Bank constructed in 1924. The Grand Banking Hall is home to several modern restaurants and bars surrounded by numerous green verdite rock columns resting on a marble floor. It is vast, extravagant and redolent of the period when London still controlled the finances of the world.

The Grapes

76 Narrow St, Limehouse, London E14 8BP

The expansion of trade

After the collapse of the South Sea Company from unbridled speculation in 1720, joint-stock companies were outlawed in Britain (an act not repealed until 1825). Even with this trade-limiting restriction, London's international trade was being compromised by a lack of adequate docking facilities. The medieval dock at Queen Hythe (still there today) was entirely unsatisfactory. Along the River Thames in the City, ships could be held up for weeks moored to the banks and stretching into the river, concertina-like. Plundering was a serious issue only held at bay by the River Police – established in 1798 and predating the Metropolitan Police by 30 years.

Bank raised £1.2 million to finance the war, with bonds promising 8 per cent annual interest. The French, not having a national debt, found it hard to compete with the English and it culminated in their defeat at the Battle of Blenheim in 1704.

The Bank of England opened for business in 1694 in Mercers' Hall in Cheapside, before moving to a classical building designed by Sir John Soane in Threadneedle Street in 1734. Only Soane's windowless exterior wall remains today, the rest being art deco

The Grapes.

The Prospect of Whitby.

Gallows at The Prospect of Whitby (replica!).

The giant West India Docks was opened in 1802 (now the Canary Wharf office complex), followed three years later by the London Dock (built 1km to east of the Tower of London) and St Katharine Docks in 1828 (now an upmarket marina) by Tower Bridge. Additional docks (e.g., East India, Wapping and Surrey) were dedicated to commodities or regions of the world. Much of the volume was due to British colonial trade, that by law had to be shipped first to London for re-distribution to other colonies – rather than permit colonies to export directly should they get any ideas above their station!

The last major developments were the Victoria (1855) and Albert (1880) docks, which saw service until Second World War bombs damaged them, and then containerisation in the 1980s which crippled London's Docklands. At a stroke hundreds of acres of land and thousands of dock-based jobs evaporated, leaving behind only deprivation and backdrops for epic films like *The Long Good Friday*. Forty years later, the London Docklands Development Corporation is regarded as having done a good job of regeneration – if maybe a tad too market driven for some.

The Grapes pub at Wapping has been serving beer on the site for nearly 500 years. Now owned by the actor Sir Ian McKellen, its river location has inspired many literary greats. It was known by the diarist Samuel Pepys, Charles Dickens described the tavern in the opening of *Our Mutual Friend* and Oscar Wilde introduces it in *The Picture of Dorian Gray*. This stretch of the Thames has a dark history, being the favoured place to drown pirates staked on the foreshore – the incoming tide providing time for some tragic personal reflection! As you'd expect from the

name, there is a generous wine list as well as delicious pub classics.

Not far from The Grapes is another very old riverside pub. The Prospect of Whitby (57 Wapping Wall, Wapping, London E1W 3SH) has been the haunt of sailors, dockworkers and smugglers since 1520 – although all that remains of the original pub is the flagstone floor. As a reminder of its dark past, a gruesome gallows and noose hang off the pub's balcony – offering a peculiar foreground to the lovely views across the river and toward the new gleaming commercial district of Canary Wharf. Judge Jeffries (the 'hanging judge'), a staunch ally of James II who sought to prevent the Glorious Revolution, was a patron – providing credibility to the gallows! You can enjoy a good selection of beer and wine alongside a serving of its famous fish and chips or a Sunday roast.

Canary Wharf.

6

GOVERNMENT

St Stephen's Tavern

10 Bridge St, London SW1A 2JJ

The legislature forms

The first English Parliament (or Great Council as it was known) was convened in 1215 with the signing of the Magna Carta by King John. This established the rights of barons – wherein the king agreed to comply with the law and would raise taxes only upon approval of his barons. But John would later achieve papal annulment of Magna Carta and his son, Henry III, continued to resist the shackles of the charter. A showdown followed in 1265, between Henry III and barons at the Battle of Lewes. The king was defeated and for 15 months Simon de Montfort and the rebel barons led the country, until their defeat (and death of de Montfort) at the Battle of Evesham in 1265 by Henry and his son – the soon-to-be King Edward I.

During his time in power, Simon de Montfort held one parliament in Westminster Hall – the medieval hall built in 1097 by King William II. The 1397 rebuild survives today, complete with an oak hammer-beam roof, and was the location of the trials of Thomas More and Charles I.

Parliament was composed of the King's Council (i.e., the Lords, namely barons and bishops) and the Commons (i.e., representatives from the towns and shires), a format that remains to this day. The Commons separated from the Lords in 1352 and remained in the Chapter House in Westminster Abbey, until both Houses co-located again in the Houses of Parliament in 1547. The Commons settled in St Stephen's Chapel, facing each other across the pews.

Despite being enemies, King Edward I adopted de Montfort's concepts and established the Model Parliament in 1295 – widely regarded as the first representative parliament. By 1362, it passed a statute decreeing that Parliament must approve all taxation – and England slowly moved into the modern era of a constitutional monarchy. Parliament voted on political unions with Wales (1540), Scotland (1707) and Ireland (1801).

When Henry VIII requisitioned Whitehall Palace from Wolsey (see page 46), he gave the fire-damaged Palace of Westminster to Parliament.

Despite the failure, in 1605, of the Gunpower Plot to assassinate the Scottish King James by blowing him and his 'Scotch beggars back to their native mountains' (according to Guy Fawkes), history repeated itself in 1834 when the 'Old Palace' went up in flames due to a basement furnace lighting up a collection of medieval 'tolly sticks' – an early form of tax receipt. The renowned English painter, J.M.W. Turner, depicted the conflagration being cheered on by a throng of spectators bidding good riddance to the controlling state.

Charles Barry and Augustus Pugin won the competition to build and furnish the new Houses of Parliament (officially the new Palace of Westminster) in the English Gothic architectural style – seen as fitting for the centre of British government. The buildings were competed in 1860, sadly with the perfectionist Pugin going insane in the process. The Elizabeth Tower (with its bell, 'Big Ben', named after a prize fighter of the day) is complemented by the even taller Victoria Tower to its south – the largest square tower in the world when built. Westminster and Lambeth bridges bookend Parliament, each painted in the colours of the Commons (red) and the Lords (green), denoting the location of each chamber.

St Stephens Tavern is Parliament's local pub (although Parliament has

St. Stephens Tavern.

Victoria Tower (Houses of Parliament).

many of its own bars). A live TV stream of proceedings and an original division bell alerts any Members of Parliament (MPs) to return and vote. Ministers such as Stanley Baldwin, Winston Churchill and Harold Macmillan are all known to have visited the pub.

The Red Lion

48 Parliament St, London SW1A 2NH

A constitutional monarchy

In 1689, following the Glorious Revolution (see page 54), a Bill of Rights was passed into law by Parliament. The bill stipulated frequent parliaments, freedom of speech within Parliament (known today as Parliamentary Privilege) and a reiteration of no taxation without approval by Parliament. (This bill was a model for other declarations including the US Bill of Rights, the United Nations Declaration of Human Rights and the European Convention on Human Rights!)

By 1721, the power of the monarch being much diluted, King George I determined that his presence was no longer required at government cabinet meetings, as had been the tradition for hundreds of years going back to the medieval Great Council. Instead, he appointed a 'Prime Minister' to provide him with weekly updates at the palace (although the first statutory reference to the role of Prime Minister was not until 1917). The king offered the post to the First Lord of the Treasury, Sir Robert Walpole, who accepted. In 1732 George II gifted Walpole a residence at 10 Downing Street – which he agreed to on the basis the property would be the 'residence in office' to all subsequent Prime Ministers. It's the system that operates today – and No. 10's door plaque still reads 'First Lord of the Treasury'. The monarch is not excluded from government – before an act of parliament passes into law it goes through the final Royal Assent and is signed by the monarch (who could in theory refuse to do so).

The Red Lion pub, so named to favour the new Scottish King James I of England in 1603, is a favourite watering hole of MPs and civil servants in Whitehall. Situated between 10 Downing Street and the Houses of Parliament, the Red Lion is the best pub in London for lovers of political intrigue. There's every chance you will spot a serving MP, made easy (in these days of permanent dress down) as the only people wearing neckties or business dress.

The Red Lion.

Downing Street.

Cenotaph, Whitehall.

The Ship and Shovell

1–3 Craven Passage, London WC2N 5PH

Tax without representation

Strapped for cash after the successful Seven Years War against France (1757–63), which cleared the way for the predominance of the British Empire, the British Parliament determined that the American colonists should pay for the large standing British military presence in North America by taxing local publications. The colonists believed that the ensuing Stamp Tax was unfair – arguing there should be 'no tax without representation' in Parliament. (At the time, neither Birmingham nor Manchester were represented in Parliament too). In any case, the colonists believed that since the French threat was expelled from North America, they didn't need British protection. Plus, they already paid taxes to their own colonial assemblies. So, they felt double-dipped. Despite the repeal of the Stamp Act the British Parliament maintained the right and authority of universal legislation over the colonies. The dispute was far from over.

Benjamin Franklin lived in Craven Street from 1757 to 1775 and acted as a lead mediator (and independent inventor and scientist) between Britain and the American colonies. Failure to sort out an acceptable tax regime led to the Declaration of Independence in 1776 and the American Wars of Independence. (Benjamin Franklin House is open to the public. One can immerse in the years where Franklin gradually ceased his support for British rule and departed to become an American revolutionary.)

Initially it was a civil war, but French support for America turned it into an international conflict – with Spain and Netherlands also supporting the United States. Ultimately, the British surrendered at Yorktown in 1781, but managed to hold on in New York City until 1783. Between 1776 to 1789 the American states were run by Congress under the Articles of the Confederation – until First President George Washington took office in 1789.

After the dust settled, John Adams became the first American Ambassador to Great Britain in 1785 (and later the second President of the United States) from the embassy at 9 Grosvenor Square (easily seen from the outside today). John Adams sought to increase foreign recognition of the United States, manging to secure 15 foreign ministers in the United States by 1788 – a major diplomatic success. However, his real objectives were the British evacuation from the western outposts, the settlement of American debts to British creditors (for work contracted before the war) and a treaty of commerce between the two nations – knotty problems never fully solved during his tenure.

The Ship and Shovell.

Benjamin Franklin House.

With this early foothold, Grosvenor Square would become central to the political, commercial and military operations of the United States in Great Britain and Europe – even being called Eisenhowerplatz during the Second World War. With the move of the US Embassy to Battersea in 2017, the modern-day association of the United States with Grosvenor Square has largely ended.

The Ship and Shovell pub is unique in London, consisting of two Grade II listed buildings on either side of a street, connected underground by a shared cellar. Established in the 1740s, its name derives from an Admiral of the Fleet. It's well known for award-winning ales by the Dorset family brewers Hall and Woodhouse. A relaxing drink at Franklin's local!

Southbank Centre

Belvedere Road, London SE1 8XX.

A tale of two Londons

Prior to 1889, London only existed as the City of London – the square mile bounded by St Paul's Cathedral in the west and the Tower of London in the east. The metropolis, outside of the City of London, was administered by the County of Middlesex, whilst urban areas south of the river were administered by the County of Surrey. The City of Westminster was part of Middlesex but governed by separate institutions of local government. This explains why the headquarters of the Middlesex County Council (now the Supreme Court) is opposite Westminster Abbey – and why the home ground of Surrey County Cricket Club is just over the River Thames in what was Surrey!

As public services grew during the nineteenth century (e.g., fire services, sanitation, transportation and housing) it became apparent that some form of London-wide authority was required to coordinate and plan the advances in infrastructure. Initially, the Metropolitan Board of Works (established in 1855) performed this role for the separate County Councils. In 1889, the concept was extended (and politicised) with the creation of the County of London – combining large parts of Middlesex and Surrey under the administration of the London County Council (LCC).

The LCC was further extended geographically in 1965 with the creation of the Greater London Council (GLC), comprising 33 boroughs and the City of London. The GLC was a powerful political force and often a thorn in the side of the Westminster government. This conflict led to its break-up in 1986, and its powers were assigned to the individual boroughs, supported (from 2000) on London-wide strategic matters by the Greater London Authority led by The Mayor of London – complementing the mayors of each borough. The mayor

South Bank Centre.

South Bank Centre.

of the City of London is the only person retaining the ancient title of Lord Mayor.

The Southbank Centre is an independent arts organisation, comprising the Royal Festival Hall, the Hayward Gallery, the Queen Elizabeth Hall and the Purcell Room, across an 11-acre site. Adjacent to it is County Hall – the former headquarters of the GLC. The Royal Festival has an excellent foyer bar, often with free live music and entertainment, plus bars with views north over the Thames.

7

CRIME AND PUNISHMENT

The Liberty Bounds

26–27 Great Tower St, London EC3R 5AQ

The Ghosts of Tower Hill

The slopes of Tower Hill have been spattered with more blue blood than any other part of London. For long the execution spot of traitors imprisoned in the nearby Tower of London, the slope running down to the river was the principal location for executions from the late fourteenth century to the 1750s – when the ghastly action (and thronging crowds) retired to Tyburn at the west end of Oxford Street and executions took on the rigorous standardisation of a production business!

Execution within the walls of the Tower was a privilege reserved for royals or those of particularly high rank – and only ten people met their end on Tower Green inside the walls. The most well-known being three queens of England: two at the behest of Henry VIII (Anne Boleyn and Catherine Howard) and the third, at the instruction of the probably reluctant Mary I, the 16-year-old Lady Jane Grey caught up in political scheming above her head – that she subsequently lost.

One of the early scalps on Tower Hill was the Archbishop of Canterbury – hacked by the mob leading the Peasants Revolt of 1381. Archbishop Simon Sudbury, advisor to Richard II, was the unfortunate 'proxy' for the king, whose 'poll tax' policies were detested. The most famous execution is that of Henry VIII's Lord Chancellor, Thomas More. More refused to sign both the 1533 Act of Succession, (recognising Anne Boleyn as the lawful queen following Henry's divorce from Catherine of Aragon) and the 1535 Act of Supremacy (recognising Henry VIII as the Supreme Head of the English Church). More was canonised in 1935 by Pope Pius XI.

More's adversary, Thomas Cromwell, Henry VIII's Chief Minister and briefly the Lord Chamberlain, followed him in 1540, for marginalising Henry in court politics and marrying him off, for geopolitical purposes, to his fifth wife Anne of Cleves – apparently not a looker!

The Liberty Bounds.

Keeping it in the family, Anne Boleyn's brother George Boleyn, and Catherine Howard's cousin Henry Howard, both met their fates on Tower Hill – George for being accused of carnal relations with his sister and Henry for getting above his station (adding the arms of King Edward the Confessor to his own coat of arms).

Edward Seymour, elder brother of Jane Seymour, beloved third queen of Henry VIII was executed in 1552 – failing to win a power struggle with John Dudley, who met the same fate two years later. As was Charles I's Archbishop of Canterbury William Laud, for pursuing a 'high church' policy, enhancing the role of priests as intermediaries in worship – and punishing any non-conformists. The puritan-led Commons charged Laud with treason and, during the Civil War, the Lords were unable to save him from the scaffold.

In total, around 100 people are believed to have been executed on Tower Hill – jeered and harangued by thousands of onlookers. The last, in 1747, was Simon Fraser, Lord Lovat – an 80-year-old Jacobite supporter of (Bonnie) Prince Charles Edward Stuart.

The Liberty Bounds is a large pub in a grand building, and part of the

Tower Bridge.

Tower Hill.

ubiquitous J.D. Wetherspoon chain. This one has the unique distinction of views of the Tower of London, Tower Hill and Tower Bridge. Upstairs, there is an extensive collection of framed prints and articles describing the history of the area – a bit of a history buff's pub!

The Viaduct Tavern

126 Newgate St, London EC1A 7AA

Hats off for the Condemned

Gaze across the road from the Viaduct Tavern and see 40,000 spectators awaiting the start of the afternoon's proceedings. Before the condemned dropped 12–18 inches, the call of 'hats off!' would be heard – not out of respect for the victim, but to ensure an unrestricted view of the poor soul's final moments! It was a sight that sickened Charles Dickens, who successfully campaigned for the abolition of public hangings – the last being in 1868. It would be another 100 years before hanging was abolished completely in 1969.

Newgate Prison followed Tyburn as the principal place of execution, exacting the death penalty for around 200 crimes and 1,200 people between 1783 and 1902. It was favoured for being next door to the Central Criminal Court (Old Bailey) – the venue for trials of London's most serious criminals – making the logistics easier than trekking to Tyburn in the west. Lesser

The Viaduct Tavern.

felons faced imprisonment (i.e., once it became a punishment after 1840) or transportation until this ceased in 1890.

'Hanging days' took place around eight times a year, seeing off five to seven people on each occasion. The trials (or Sessions) at the adjacent court ran to the same frequency and the executions took place about six weeks after the trial. For 100 years until 1832, medical science advanced with the bodies of the executed being publicly anatomised at Surgeon's Hall.

Newgate Prison was finally demolished in 1904. New modern prisons sprung up at London's Millbank, Pentonville and Holloway, practicing the new 'penitentiary system' – a long term stay with forced exercise on the treadmill. In its place, the new Central Criminal Court opened in 1907 and is operating to the present day.

The Viaduct Tavern is the last surviving Gin Palace in London, opening the same year that public executions ceased and the construction of the nearby Holborn Viaduct. It is an elegant, curved Grade II listed building with a stunning interior – particularly its Victorian etched glass panels. A Fuller's pub serving the range of house ales and many local and imported beers too. Built above the old Newgate Prison, they might give you a peek at one of the old cells if you ask!

The Ten Bells

84 Commercial St, London E1 6QQ

The ghastly summer of '88

Infamous as being the most shocking and revolting of all serial murderers in London, Jack the Ripper was appropriately named, his hallmark being a slit throat and horrific bodily mutilation. The murders happened over three autumn months in 1888 in the Whitechapel area of London. Despite the enormous attention the case received, and the efforts of numerous amateur sleuths, no one knows who the culprit was – the paucity of evidence is only matched by the abundance of theories. What we do know is the murderer made havoc of the investigation by exploiting the rivalries between the 'City of London Police' and the 'Metropolitan Police' – who were highly competitive and uncooperative with each other.

The Ripper's victims were all (bar one) prostitutes, probably soliciting at the time of their deaths. At least two had fallen to alcoholism and used prostitution to pay for their addiction. Martha Turner was probably the first victim on 7 August 1888. Mary Ann Nicholls and Annie Chapman (separated by a few weeks) were next; sad circumstances had led Annie falling from being a vet's wife and mother to an alcoholic.

The Ten Bells.

Elizabeth Stride was the fourth victim and her story is perhaps the most tragic. Her entire family had died ten years earlier when the *Princess Alice* steamer sank on the River Thames in the worst ever British inland waterway shipping accident, claiming 600–700 poor souls.

Catherine Eddowes was victim number five, followed sometime later by the Ripper's last known victim Mary Jane Kelly on 9 November. Hers was the only indoor murder; privacy and time permitting the most troubling and abominable mutilations. In a vain attempt to uncover the likeness of her killer, her eyes were photographed in the hope they might record some final images.

At the junction of Commercial Street and Fournier Street is the Ten Bells pub – a known drinking den of some of the Ripper's victims and probably the perpetrator himself. The pub was built in 1851 and is Grade II listed. Aside its faded décor and candlelit ambience, lending to its ghoulish claim to fame, there are very attractive murals commemorating the silk weaving heritage of nearby Spitalfields.

The Star Tavern

6 Belgrave Mews W, London SW1X 8HT

The new highwaymen

On 8 August 1963 a 15-man gang held up the London bound Royal Mail train from Glasgow, netting £2.6m in used notes, a record haul for the time – but achieved by meting out a severe injury to one the guards, resulting in life-long brain damage. The so-called Great Train Robbery was the escapade planned by the gang's ringleader Bruce Reynolds, a known burglar and armed robber. The robbery was well executed, but the subsequent hideout and getaway were botched, leading to the early apprehension of twelve of the gang. Reynolds was captured within five years and another, Ronnie Biggs (with the aid of plastic surgery), made a new life in Brazil and held out until 2001 when he returned of his own accord. One gang member was never caught, having successfully hidden his identity from everyone.

In the run up to the robbery, the gang met at the Star Tavern in Belgravia – a favourite haunt of 1960s upmarket gangsters and cat burglars – the term describing the modus operandi of Peter Scott, suspected of stealing £200,000 of jewellery from Sophia Loren in 1960. The pub and the first-floor dining room where the some of the gang met, hasn't changed much. Situated in upmarket Belgravia it had a reputation as a place where stars (such as Diana Dors, Peter O'Toole, Albert Finney and Alexander Korda) took a bizarre pleasure from quaffing Dom Perignon with gentleman robbers.

The Star Tavern, in common with all pubs in Belgravia, is in a mews – a

The Star Tavern.

Mews Courtyard, west London.

street comprising stables, coach houses and servants' accommodation for the attached grand property. The mews operated under a strict hierarchy, headed by the Head Coachman, supported by grooms and stableboys. Wages were low (and leave consisted of one day per month), partly due to the inclusion of board and lodgings, but also the absence of any welfare system meant the alternative was the workhouse. By the pub's open fire downstairs, one can visualise the Head Coachman and liveried grooms supping a pint whilst poring over the day's tribulations.

Did you know: the word mews derives from medieval times as an area where hunting hawks were kept whilst moulting – making a shrieking 'mewing' sound whilst doing so. Each mews property fetches millions in Belgravia today!

8

DESTRUCTION

The Ship

11 Talbot Court, London EC3V 0BP

The City in ruins

'Anybody could wee it out', to paraphrase Thomas Blood the Lord Mayor on seeing Pudding Lane alight. Words he would regret, as the wind fanned the flames westwards that Sunday morning on 2 September 1666. The ensuing conflagration eventually claimed 13,000 houses, 88 churches, 44 livery company halls, key civic buildings (e.g., the Royal Exchange and the Guildhall) and most tragically the medieval St. Paul's Cathedral (see page 24). Starting in Pudding Lane and ending at Pie Corner it was assumed to be a visitation from the Lord for the sins of gluttony, profanity (in nearby Billingsgate Fish Market) and prostitution (in Drury Lane).

Fires were common in the seventeenth century when homes were made of timber and constructed of floors that jettied out – making it easy for fires (starting on the ground floor) to rise through the building. The source of the fire was Thomas Farriner's bakery where it's likely the oven had not been fully extinguished and sparks set fire to some nearby flour. A combination of circumstances led to the spread of the fire, including a preceding summer-long drought, a strong easterly wind (a westerly would have funnelled the fire into the river) and a rudimentary fire service that did not operate on Sundays. Inaction to prevent the spread of the fire was eventually overcome when the King, Charles II, and his younger brother James, instructed the creation of a fire break by dynamiting some rows of houses. After four days, having started in Pudding Lane, the fire burned itself out at Pie Corner – lending credence to the belief the Lord had shown his displeasure of gluttons. The homeless moved to friends or relatives in the west, many never to return, whilst others camped out in the hills of Hampstead and Highgate to the north.

A monument to the Great Fire was completed in 1677. Designed by Christopher Wren and Robert Hooke (the same team that rebuilt St Paul's) and standing 202 feet high, it remains the world's tallest Doric column (other high monuments tend to be obelisks). Topped with a gilded urn, its construction caused more deaths than the fire itself. Sadly, it also would become a favoured location for suicides until a cage was added in 1850. A plaque at the base by C. Gabriel Cibber provides a before and after representation of the fire – calling attention to figures representing the City of London, Father Time, the King, his brother – and goddesses of Peace and Plenty promising better times ahead. Catholics were initially blamed for starting the fire – fuelled by a hapless Catholic Frenchman who

claimed responsibility and was swiftly despatched by the authorities – a plaque claiming the fire was the work of a Catholic plot was eventually removed in 1831!

The Ship pub is easily missed, tucked away in one of the City's many alleyways. The original pub fell victim to the Great Fire and this seventeenth-century rebuild is a small pub with a period spiral staircase leading to an additional upstairs bar. The large outside courtyard ensures it is filled with City workers in the milder months. In common with some of the longer standing traditional City pubs it is closed at the weekends.

The Ship.

The Seven Stars

53 Carey St, London WC2A 3QS

Rebuilding the City

With 80 per cent of the City in ashes, it was obvious there would need to be a total rebuild. Temporary buildings were erected, but the lack of proper sanitation and harsh winter weather led to disease and death. Victims of the fire struggled with each other to claim the boundaries of their former properties and many set about rebuilding almost immediately. Parliament quickly appointed a court consisting of 22 eminent Fire Judges to rule and arbitrate over property disputes between Landlords and tenants of burnt buildings. Parliament also passed the Act for the Rebuilding of the City of London in February 1667. It required that all new buildings were constructed of stone or brick and should not jetty out in the traditional style that aimed to increase floor space in upper floors – but became so packed in that one could shake hands with neighbours opposite. It would also outlaw 'knocking through' one building into the next that had been common with families.

Within a week of the fire abating, at the invitation of King Charles II, Christopher Wren and John Evelyn (the writer and diarist) submitted separate designs – both utilising a grid pattern and intending to rival the baroque style found in Paris. Other eminent scientists and engineers followed suit, without invitation. Ultimately though, it was to no avail as people eagerly started to re-build their properties on the old street-plan and the government wasn't willing to force (and its new rebuilding Coal Tax wouldn't pay for) a grand new city design. Some roads were widened and narrow alleyways removed – but only two new roads were added: King Street leading into Queen street – both running south from Guildhall. Part of the fascination and impact of the City today is the juxtaposition of a medieval street pattern and modern buildings.

The experience of the fire also accelerated the demand for, and professionalism of, fire insurance to indemnify for losses due to fire. It was the catalyst that led to the world's first insurance company, established by Nicholas Barbon in 1667. Insured homes would display a plaque to mark them out to the company-run fire services.

In addition to rebuilding St Paul's Cathedral, the office of Wren played the main role in rebuilding most of the City's churches, believed to be around 52 buildings. Many perished in the Blitz of the Second World War, but some magnificent examples still stand, including: St Martin without Ludgate, St Stephen Walbrook, St Bride's Church and St Dunstan in the East (bombed out in the war and now an outdoor micro-climate haven).

The compact Seven Stars pub is one of the few buildings to survive the Great

The Seven Stars.

Fire. Dating from 1602, it's a favourite of lawyers working at the nearby Inns of Court and the Royal Courts of Justice (which it pre-dates by nearly 300 years) and a worthy candidate for being London's oldest pub. It has a good range of ales, bar snacks and food, but little space, so avoid busy times unless that's the experience you're after.

The Old Bell Tavern

95 Fleet St, Greater, London EC4Y 1DH

Blood, sweat and tears

By the summer of 1940, Hitler's planned invasion of Britain (Operation Sea Lion) was in full preparation. But first, Hitler needed air superiority over the English Channel. This meant destroying RAF airfields in the south of England and the sources of aircraft production throughout the country. The enemy attacks started on 10 July 1940 and continued every day throughout summer – and so the Battle of Britain commenced. During the first six weeks, and despite the heroic efforts of hundreds of air crew, Britain was losing the battle – aircraft production and training couldn't keep up with the loses of pilots and aircraft.

The break happened on 24 August 1940. A Luftwaffe pilot got lost and 'accidentally' bombed the east end, near the City of London. The following night Churchill gave orders for the bombing of Berlin. It was fateful but viewed as strategically necessary. Churchill knew that Hitler would likely retaliate by bombing London – and this would have two (calculated) side effects. Firstly, it would draw fire away from British airfields and factories, allowing some recovery time, and secondly the sight of London in flames may produce the political imperative for the United States to enter the war.

The Blitz of London itself commenced on 7 September 1940 and ran for 57 consecutive nights. Initial raids focused on the east end of London. Despite a widespread blackout, German bombers were able to follow the outline of the 'Isle of Dogs' – and St Paul's Cathedral marked the destination. Raids targeted telephone exchanges, railway stations and industrial locations. On this evening, there were two raids: one at 4 p.m. and another at 8 p.m. Around 320 bombers and 600 enemy fighters took part that night – described as looking like 'hundreds of birds heading to the docks'. It was a dreadful path of destruction up the river Thames and into London – killing 450 people across London that night. But Churchill's strategy worked. Gradually factories replaced aircraft faster than losses and British and allied pilots defeated the Luftwaffe, aided by the superior Spitfire fighter.

Hitler gave up Operation Sea Lion during October 1940 to concentrate his efforts on Operation Barbarossa (the invasion of Russia). The heavy bombing of London was to continue – but only as an attempt to reduce the morale of the British people. The principal target was St Paul's Cathedral. It became a national priority to ensure St Paul's was saved and hundreds of fire-fighters maintained round-the-clock surveillance and firefighting operations.

The worst night of bombing was 29 December 1940. Whilst fatalities were lower, destruction to the City of London was more significant from estimated 25,000 incendiary bombs causing widespread fire. On top of 28 major fires and 1,400 smaller fires there were six conflagrations. In the City this included the Guildhall, three Livery Halls and six medieval churches.

The worst hit areas were the docklands and buildings around St Paul's Cathedral. In particular Shoe Lane off Fleet Street, which suffered complete destruction. Around half of Wren's post-Great Fire churches were destroyed in the Blitz – some rebuilt, some with only towers remaining (Christ Church Greyfriars and St Dunstan in the East) and others lost forever. But importantly, St Paul's was saved.

The Blitz of London had lasted from 7 September 1940 to 10 May 1941, and there had been 32,000 deaths across London. In the ancient (medieval) City

The Old Bell Tavern.

of London, 25 per cent of dwellings, 18 churches and 17 Livery Halls were destroyed.

The Old Bell, opposite Shoe Lane, survived the Blitz. It's another of London's oldest pubs, having been licensed for some 300 years. The pub is believed to have been a favourite of Wren's stonemasons, working on St Paul's and the adjacent St Bride's Church (today, known as the journalists' church due to Fleet Street's newspaper publishing heritage). There is an external alleyway at the rear where one can gaze up at the steeple of St Bride's – one of Wren's finest works and said to be the inspiration for a local baker to produce the tiered design of wedding cakes. Inside, there is a good selection of local ales and food.

9

EXPANSION

Lamb & Flag

33 Rose St, London WC2E 9EB

London moves west

From the early 1600s pollution and the risk of fire in the City of London encouraged a steady drift of well-to-dos seeking the fresh air and safety found in the west. A favoured site was Covent Garden, originally a medieval orchard and garden belonging to the Convent of the Church of St Peter at Westminster (Westminster Abbey). With the dissolution of the monasteries from 1536, King Henry VIII gave the land to one of his supporters, John Russell, 1st Earl of Bedford, and the first 'n' of Convent was dropped in the process!

A few generations later, in 1630, Francis Russell, 4th Earl of Bedford, commissioned Inigo Jones to build a residential square (probably following the fashion set in Paris ten years earlier at Place des Vosges). Derided at the time for its Italianate design, it became London's first high-end residential square. In 1670 a Royal Charter was granted for a fruit, vegetable and flower market – to 'hold forever a market in the Piazza on every day in the year except Sundays and Christmas Day for the buying and selling of all manner of fruit, flowers, roots and herbs'.

St Paul's Church, Covent Garden was built by Inigo Jones in 1633 and consecrated in 1638. Lord Bedford (not being a religious man) said 'it should be no more than a barn'. Jones replied, 'it'll be the handsomest barn in England'. In fact, it's modelled on a Roman temple – the first English church of that style, and only 100 years after the Reformation when England turned its back on the Roman church.

After some promising early years, the area went into decline from the 1740s. Cheaper house prices encouraged London's artistic community to take up residence, but over time it became the favoured haunt of drunks, the destitute and prostitutes. Between 1757–95 there was even a guide to the local call-girls named *Harris's Covent Garden Ladies*!

The circle turned and regeneration started in 1830 when a Victorian market was built, surviving as a

Lamb & Flag.

wholesale market until 1972 – and still standing today as the large stone central market. Alfred Hitchcock used the market as the location for his 1972 film, *Frenzy*.

Today, Covent Garden is home to the world-renowned Royal Opera House, the Royal Ballet and the London Transport Museum – as well as some of the best shopping, food & drink and street entertainment in London.

Another claimant to London's oldest pub is the seventeenth century Lamb & Flag. A pub is believed to have been on this site since 1623. Tucked at the end of an alleyway and boasting a small courtyard (a location for bareknuckle fighting in less gentrified times) it's a very popular pub – ideal for a refreshment after visiting Covent Garden. Patrons have included Dickens and the poet John Dryden – apparently the victim of an attempted murder in the courtyard in 1679. The pub interior is faithful to its period with plenty of wood panelling and a narrow wooden staircase to the upstairs rooms. The pub features a wide range of beers and drinks and traditional English pub cooking, including popular Sunday roasts.

Covent Garden Market.

The Blue Posts

22 Berwick St, London W1F 0QA

Expansion under the Stuarts

Soho has seen multiple transformations since its conception in the late seventeenth century – from parkland to an aristocratic and diplomatic quarter, then a refuge for diverse European communities. Today, it's one of London's most vibrant entertainment areas.

Soho is thought to take its name from the hunting cries used when it was a royal hunting park belonging to King Henry VIII who hunted here with members of his court and the aristocracy. Soho is bounded by four major thoroughfares, including Oxford Street (to the north) and Regent Street (to the west).

Records from medieval times point to Soho being church land owned by the Abbot of Abingdon and home to a leper hospital. After its 'acquisition' by King Henry VIII, its proximity to Whitehall Palace made it popular for hunting.

Later in the Tudor and Stuart periods, the royal land was sold or granted to aristocrats and the wealthy. The principal resident of 'Soho Fields' at this time was the Duke of Monmouth, the illegitimate son of King Charles II. (The Duke came to his end on Tower Hill for taking on his Catholic uncle King James II.) The Earl of Leicester was another key resident.

From around 1660, landowners and property developers such as Wardour, Frith and Jermyn developed the area – honouring themselves and the Bishop of London, Dean Henry Compton, in the street names. The Great Fire made their investment very timely and profitable. The fashionable residential squares at the time were Soho Square (1680) and Golden Square (1700) – both of which still exist today but only a few of the original homes survive, being replaced by Georgian and Victorian buildings.

Soho was eventually eclipsed by Mayfair (to the west) and became home to many immigrants, the source of its cultural diversity today. French Huguenots, Greeks and Italians all established roots – in cramped, rudimentary and over-filled homes. (The Chinese community did not arrive in Soho until after the Second World War, coming from Limehouse in east London owing to the bombing and widespread destruction of their dwellings.)

An outbreak of Cholera in 1854 marked an end to wealthier families living in Soho. They too moved west to Mayfair or south into newer areas like Belgravia. At this point, Soho started to develop its niche as an area for entertainment. Many theatres, music halls and drinking establishments sprang up. The decline of domestic service after the First World War also gave rise to numerous restaurants.

The Blue Posts.

Popular music was another key ingredient in Soho, introduced by Americans, after the Second World War. Along with music, Soho also became home to the fashion and film industries in surrounding offices, still used today by a multitude of media companies. After some difficult times caused by organised crime and prostitution in the 1960s and 1970s, Soho has once again established itself as one of London's most exciting, diverse and culturally integrated areas.

The Blue Posts pub derives its name from the two posts placed outside taverns in the eighteenth century where Sedan Chairs would park, awaiting custom. Singled out here since it's a pub that has stayed true to its roots, presenting something of a time warp back to 60s London. The interior and bar are adorned with brewery signage from the period. An active events agenda brings it screaming to the modern age with regular cabaret sessions and blues and jazz jams. (NB: Not to be mistaken for the pub of the same name in nearby Rupert Street – a more upmarket but less earthy experience!)

Ye Grapes

16 Shepherd Market, London W1J 7QQ

Stuart Mayfair

Mayfair, named after its raucous annual fair, was purpose-built during the mid-1700s. Many wealthy residents moved here from Covent Garden – where their descendants had settled after the devastating Great Fire (see page 87).

Sir Richard Grosvenor engaged Thomas Barlow to lay out Mayfair around three large squares: Berkeley Square, Hanover Square and Grosvenor Square. Sir Richard inherited the land from his father, Sir Thomas Grosvenor – who had acquired it upon his marriage to Mary Davies, heiress to 500 acres of central London. Today, the Grosvenor Estate still owns swathes of Mayfair – making the current young Duke of Westminster a very wealthy man.

The 'Mayfair' itself ran from 1686 to 1764, before it was supressed by the area's new residents. Surprisingly, they didn't take to the annual visit of showmen, jugglers, prize-fighters, semolina eating contests, prostitutes and copious cheap ale on their doorstep!

Piccadilly, which bounds the south side, was originally the medieval high road to Reading. By the 1500s, Piccadilly was a thriving fashion centre, taking its name from the ruff lace collars ('Piccadills') that were manufactured in workshops along the street. Piccadilly's north side was lined with the London homes of the country's landed gentry, of which the most important were Burlington House, Cambridge House, Albany House and Devonshire House (all but Devonshire House still stand).

Edward Shepherd's 1735 market was a focal point of the 'Mayfair' until it was abolished in 1764 – the market buildings we see today were built in 1860. Around Shepherd Market is a 'Blue Plaque' (i.e., official plaques that identify former homes of the famous) paradise. Nearby, in Chesterfield Street, number 4 was home to George Bryan 'Beau' Brummell. A society wit and good friend of the Prince Regent, he was famed as an arbiter of men's fashion and among the first to wear tailored jackets and trousers – as opposed to the loose-fitting garments and stockings of the time. Sadly, later in life, he ran up gambling debts and fell out with his old friend (by then King George IV) – dying of neurosyphilis in social exile in Caen. Another famous resident was Anthony Eden, remembered for his ill-judged British imperial efforts to oust President Nasser of Egypt in the 1956/7 Suez Crisis – pretty much the dying gasp of the British Empire.

The visitor is spoilt for choice in Shepherd Market. Its tucked-away location makes it a sanctuary away from day-trippers and tourists. The many Victorian-period pubs include Ye Grapes, The King's Arms, The Market Tavern and The Chesterfield Arms.

Ye Grapes.

Home of Beau Brummell and Anthony Eden.

Perhaps Ye Grapes has the edge, historically, quenching the thirsts of market workers continuously since it was established in in the mid-1700s (present building 1882). It's also situated in a courtyard that hosts throngs of locals in summer.

The Grenadier

18 Wilton Row, London SW1X 7NR

London moves further west

As Londoners moved west following the Great Fire, first to Covent Garden and Soho, then to Mayfair in the eighteenth century, they landed on Belgravia in the nineteenth century. Each move corresponded to fresher air, more tranquillity and space.

Today, Belgravia is home to many foreign embassies and wealthy residents, based around the centrepiece of Belgrave Square – a large, leafy and secluded private garden for the officials of the embassies and residents of the square.

In 1677, the 200-acre plot was acquired by Sir Thomas Grosvenor upon his marriage to Mary Davies (the niece of Hugh Audley, who had purchased the land from the monarchy in the early 1600s). This added to his already impressive 100-acre plot in Mayfair. And today, the Grosvenor family still own these 300 acres of prime London real estate, valued at around £10 billion.

A catalyst for the transformation was the conversion of nearby Buckingham House (or The Queen's House as it was renamed by George III) to Buckingham Palace by King George IV, starting in 1820. This gave a lift to the area and an associated opportunity for property development, seized upon by Sir Robert Grosvenor, the 1st Marquess of Westminster.

A strategic plan was drawn up to convert the marshy (clay-rich) land into a vast high-end residential estate. The work started in 1820 and continued for nearly 40 years. Ingeniously, the underlying clay was used to make bricks on site and the fill-in was spoil from the excavation of St Katharine Docks in the City happening over the same period. Nearly all the buildings are covered in 'stucco'; fine plaster painted white.

Sir Robert Grosvenor hired Thomas Cundy as the chief designer and Thomas Cubitt as the chief builder. Cubitt became enormously successful by adopting the concept and role of the 'prime contractor'. Many of the streets in Belgravia are named after the towns and villages of Grosvenor's Cheshire Estate: Belgrave, Eccleston,

Chester and the family seat of Eaton Hall. Today, Belgravia is tightly managed so you won't find many shops, no buses pass through and the pubs are hidden in the former mews of the grand homes.

In Wilton Place, St Paul's Church (1843) was the first in London to champion the Oxford Movement; a group that sought adoption of 'High Church' practices by the Anglican faith. Also seek out the plaque on the north side of the church commemorating 39 women who served as part of the female Special Operations Executive (SOE), bravely operating on occupied French soil in the Second World War. The Croix de Guerre next to their names signifies those who died in action. The SOE women were drawn from the Women's Transport Service (WTS) for their language skills, family ties in France and true grit.

Around the corner in Motcomb Street, the Pantechnicon towers over the pedestrianised street. Originally built as a store for works of art in the 1820s, this building gave its name to the large vans that moved art and furniture around the world for wealthy Brits and foreign embassy officials.

The Grenadier can claim to be one of London's most difficult-to-find pubs. One again, located in a mews (see page 86), it is behind St Paul's Church in Wilton Row. It was built in 1720 as an officer's mess for the First

The Grenadier.

Buckingham Palace.

Foot Guards – the Duke of Wellington played cards with fellow officers on the first floor. Barracks were added in 1750 at the back of the pub, replaced by the present-day cottages and stables in 1826. After the Battle of Waterloo in 1815, the guards were re-named the Grenadier Guards, today one of the five foot-regiments of the King's Household Division. Featuring a pewter-topped bar, The Grenadier is popular with well-heeled clientele and personalities – safe in the knowledge that the wealthy locals don't tend to seek autographs!

The Guinea

30 Bruton Pl, London W1J 6NL

Wealthy, on the move again

To the west of Shepherd Market lies Berkeley Square. Once the garden of Devonshire House, the London home of successive Dukes of and Duchesses of Devonshire, as portrayed by the famous 5th Duke and Duchess in the film *The Duchess*. Devonshire House was originally named Berkeley House after Lord Berkeley of Stratton, remodelled by the architect William Kent in 1733 and finally demolished in 1924 – making way for the new house of the same name facing Piccadilly. The London Plane trees in the square are the original ones, planted in 1733.

Berkeley Square is home to some splendid original houses from the period, including a fascinating trio at 44–46 Berkeley Square. The architectural historian, Nikolaus Pevsner, described the property at no. 44 (also by William Kent) as the finest terrace house in London – it's now an exclusive club. Number 45 Berkeley Square is the former home of 'Clive of India'. Robert Clive was a soldier who led a militarised British East India Company to victory over the French equivalent at the Battle of Plassey in 1757 – each army supported by their selected Indian allies. The battle helped the British East India Company take control of Bengal and was the foundation for subsequent British rule in all of India until Indian Independence in 1947. Clive amassed

The Guinea.

Berkeley Square.

a fortune in plunder and gifts from Indian rulers (as a commissioned officer this was the established method of fiscal gain before the introduction of a professional army). Upon his return to London, he commissioned this house. Criticised for his part in the death of around 10 million Indian citizens in the Bengal famine of 1770, he committed suicide in 1774. The famous Annabel's Club occupies 46 Berkeley Square – the club's external seasonal decorations make a spectacular impact.

The Guinea pub dates from 1675, although it claims origins further back when the area was farmland and the pub was frequented by farm workers. More recently it's well-known for The Guinea Grill, specialising in steaks and befitting its farming heritage.

10

DISEASE AND ILLNESS

The Walrus and Carpenter

45 Monument St, London EC3R 8BU

Bring out your dead

In the year 1665, you were lucky to die peacefully of old age. Of 97,306 deaths recorded by the Clerk's Office of the City of London, only 1,845 died of old age. Many died of the usual illnesses understood at the time – but a thumping 68,596 deaths were attributed to the Great Plague. Adding in deaths outside the City parishes, it's thought the total was probably around 100,000. And other areas of the country were badly affected too.

For six months (from spring to the late autumn), it was a deadly and desperate time to be in London. The King, royal court and the wealthy had fled. Some principled doctors remained to try and prevent death (using what we would regard as quack methods today) by rebalancing the four humours of the body (i.e., black bile, yellow bile, blood and phlegm) – thought to be causing the disease brought on by the inhalation of foul air. Doctors would wear beak shaped 'nosegays' stuffed with herbs and spices to prevent inhalation of the so-called miasma.

The plague had landed on London every 11 years since 1603, but 1665 was its most devasting and final visitation – believed to be divine intervention for breaking the Sabbath and for blasphemy. Today, we know the plague was carried by fleas living on rats – attracted to the waste and decay readily found in the streets. A bite from an infected flea was all it took to contract the bubonic plague – named after the blackened 'buboes' that would appear around the body's lymphatic systems. In their misguided wisdom, the authorities had ordered the destruction of many thousands of cats and dogs – the rats had the place to themselves.

The plague caused a painful death for around 25 per cent of sufferers, as you lived through your decomposing body. But most could survive if young and healthy enough to fight the infection. Doors locked and a red cross painted on your door, the only lifeline was the daily food and water provided by parish officials and prayers that you would survive the 40-day quarantine

The Walrus and Carpenter.

period. Looking down Lovat Lane it's easy to visualise the cart drivers calling out 'bring out your dead'. Many were buried in plague pits, like the one still intact at St Mary at Hill at the top of the lane – apparent by the raised ground in the church's courtyard. The King returned in early February 1665, and London quickly got back to business – oblivious to the impending destruction coming later in the year, as disastrous to property as the plague had been to life.

Standing outside the Walrus and Carpenter pub is a perfect location to gaze up the cobbled paving of Lovat Lane at the Tudor-style buildings and admire the full height of Wren and Hooke's Fire of London Monument to the west. There is a very good selection of drinks, specialising in cask ales and gins.

John Snow

39 Broadwick St, London W1F 9QJ

Airborne or waterborne?
Soho's reputation as a desirable place to live was well and truly tarnished in 1854 at the outbreak of a cholera epidemic – a periodic illness that spreads quickly in densely populated areas. It was little understood at the time, and physicians had no idea what

John Snow.

caused the illness, other than believing it was airborne. The sufferer would be unable to hold anything down and death was caused by dehydration.

John Snow began working as a physician in 1837, specialising in medical hygiene. Challenged by the case, he mapped the incidence of illness in Soho and was able to narrow down the source of infection. The break came when an elderly woman in Hampstead contracted the illness. Snow spoke with her and learned she formerly lived in Soho and preferred to fetch her drinking water from the Broad Street pump in Soho – correlating closely to Snow's mapping. Snow quickly realised the significance. Believing cholera to be airborne, the authorities were reluctant to remove the pump handle – so Snow did it himself and observed the decline in cases. The root cause was determined to be sewage that had seeped into the drinking water system. London eventually gripped the problem of public sanitation and cross-borough coordination by establishing the Metropolitan Board of Works a year later in 1855.

The John Snow pub (specialising in ales by the brewer Sam Smith) commemorates Snow's achievement, although he was a teetotaller until his last years. In keeping with its Victorian heritage, the ground floor is portioned into separate drinking areas. A replica of the pump stands outside the pub.

11

INFRASTRUCTURE

The Hoop & Grapes

47 Aldgate High St, London EC3N 1AL

The wall and gates of London

It took around 85,000 tons of Kentish ragstone to construct the two-miles long London Wall. Impressive, particularly when we consider this was courtesy of the Romans in around AD220. Built for the dual purpose of defence and customs collection it survived until the late middle ages defining the boundary of the City of London – a horseshoe shape around the City with the river on its southside. Adding to its defensive capability was the River Fleet on its western boundary and later (in 1070AD under the Normans) the Tower of London would bolster its eastern flank. The most impressive remains are at Cooper's Row (in the east) and Cripplegate (in the north). Cooper's Row also displays a replica monument bearing the inscription of Julius Classicianus, procurator of Britain, who brought peace after the Boudican rebellion of AD60 (see page 9) – the original can be seen in the British Museum. There were

seven gates passing through London Wall – all built by the Romans except the medieval Moorgate. All the gates were demolished between 1760–62 to make way for road traffic.

Working clockwise, first there is Ludgate, thought to have been built to provide access to burial grounds outside the City in the area that is Fleet Street and Strand today. Traditionally believed to be named after King Lud (a Celtic King) in 66BC, it is now adorned with a statue of Queen Elizabeth I, now removed to nearby St Dunstan in the West. Newgate was built to provide a route to Roman Silchester and Bath and St Albans (via Watling Street). Aldersgate was associated with the nearby Roman Fort – garrison for 1,000 troops built after the Boudican Revolt. Cripplegate provided a route north, and later led to the London Charterhouse, Clerkenwell and Islington. It is thought to have been named after its popularity among cripples to receive donations aided by the church just outside the wall: St Giles without Cripplegate. St Giles is the burial place of poet and minister in Cromwell's government, John Milton. It's also where Cromwell

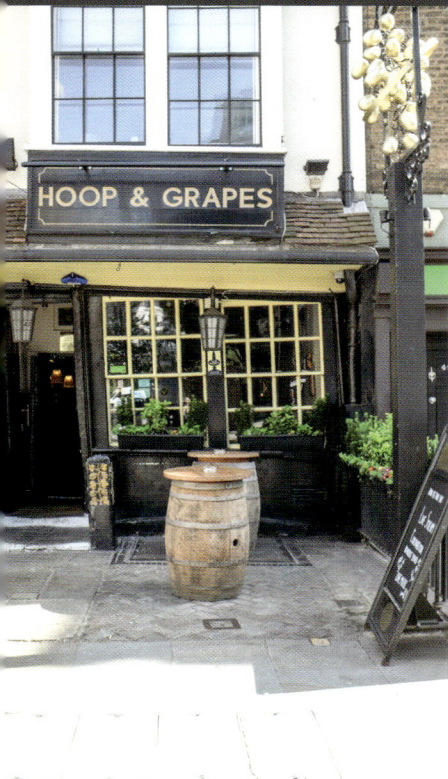

The Hoop & Grapes.

Lloyd's of London.

was married in 1620 at the age of 21. Moorgate was built in 1415, leading to the marshy Moorfields – and is now a key centre of banking, insurance and home of the Chartered Institute of Accountants. Bishopsgate, as the name suggests, led to the bishoprics of Lincoln and York and home to Sir Thomas Gresham (see page 60). Finally, Aldgate led to the Roman road network toward Essex and East Anglia via Stratford and Colchester and was home to Geoffrey Chaucer in the 1370s.

The Hoop and Grapes is a very old pub – claiming to be the oldest licensed premises in London. It is a rare timber building, now leaning towards the east, that survived the Great Fire (see page 60) – and consequently is Grade II listed. Timber beams, sash windows, sloping floors and low ceilings create the most authentic Tudor pub experience in London. Originally named the Hops and Grapes to advertise availability of beer and wines, today a wide range of food and drink is available.

The George

75 Borough High St, London SE1 1NH

Bridging the Thames

For nearly 1,500 years there was a single bridge crossing the River Thames in London. This was London Bridge – first established by the Romans in AD50 at a narrow section of the river, between two defensive hills (Ludgate Hill and Cornhill) and serviced by the fresh water River Walbrook. More than a thousand years later (in 1176) a stone bridge was built by the architect Peter de Colechurch under the instruction of Henry II (to also rest the body of Thomas Becket).

Concerns over defence, loss of tolls, loss of fees to ferrymen and obstruction to river-based traffic all conspired to stop further bridge building until the congestion on Old London Bridge made the case overwhelming. In 1729 a timber bridge was eventually constructed at Putney and the ferrymen's claims of consequential losses were paid. It was followed by Westminster Bridge (1750), Blackfriars (1769) and Battersea (1772) – although none of the originals survive today. The medieval London Bridge was demolished in 1832. Today there are 35 road, rail and foot bridges crossing the Thames between Hampton Court Bridge and Tower Bridge – the oldest

The George.

Borough Market, Southwark.

bridge dates from 1860 (Grosvenor Rail Bridge). Plus, several tunnels – including the world's first tunnel under a river at Wapping: Marc Brunel's Thames Tunnel, built in 1843.

The Thames in London was once a tidal marshland about 1km wide, divided by central islands. Today, successive engineering works and land reclamation have turned the Thames into a fast-flowing canal – accounting for it no longer freezing over as it regularly did in medieval times (partly due to the slowing effect of the 18 arches of Old London Bridge).

Seventy kilometres downstream the Thames emerges into the sea, mapping directly onto the River Rhine 150km to the east, the ancient route used by the Romans to trade with the most western part of the Roman Empire.

The George in Southwark (an area named by the Romans to distinguish the 'south work' on the opposite side of the bank to the main settlement) is one of London's most historic, original and atmospheric pubs. The pub dates from 1583, but today's incarnation as a coaching inn from the late seventeenth century is immediately apparent. Both traders and passengers would set off south from The George having replenished stocks from the market opposite (today, the popular Borough

Church of St Mary Axe.

Market). Not only was Dickens a patron, giving the establishment a mention in *Little Dorrit*, but Shakespeare performed his plays in the courtyard to the audience in the balconies. And in the fourteenth century, Chaucer set the beginning of *The Canterbury Tales* in the shared courtyard with the long-gone Tabard pub. The George is London's last remaining galleried inn and the only pub in London to be owned by the National Trust. Complementing a good selection of local ales, craft beers and gin are pub classics like scotch eggs, chicken wings and devilled whitebait.

The Euston Tap

190 Euston Rd, London NW1 2EF

Railway mania

Brutal. The only way to describe the steam hammers, bulldozers and gangs of labourers that marched their way through London, laying down rail tracks, closing in on the centre, displacing thousands of residents and slum dwellers in the process and exacerbating the already desperate overcrowding. After ten years of destruction a Royal Commission decreed in 1846 that railways should not penetrate the inner-city area. Eventually 12 termini were built circling the capital around two miles from the centre in all directions.

By the 1830s, throughout the country, canal systems were being replaced by the new steam-powered rail technology, first proven in 1808 by Richard Trevithick and commercialised in 1825 by the Stephensons' father and son team, between Stockton and Darlington. Primarily conceived for freight movements, it wasn't long before 'railway mania' took off with the public seeking some of the adventure, exhilaration and opportunity presented by high-speed travel. The London and Greenwich Railway was first to reach London in 1836, with its terminus at London Bridge. Expanding horizons a year later, Robert Stephenson designed the 112-mile-long London to Birmingham Railway (also comprising 150 bridges, 17 stations, 8 tunnels and 5 viaducts!). The line terminated at Euston Station – making it London's first mainline terminus, and the world's first long distance inter-city railway. This was the age of Victorian confidence, ambition and sheer bloody-mindedness!

The arrival of the railways changed London. Faster journey times north/south, the age of the commuter, exotic new products from home and abroad and the urbanisation of areas such as Richmond, Croydon and Slough (for the wealthy) and Putney, Ealing and Kilburn (for artisans and clerks).

By 1852, the country was saturated with around 7,000 miles of track. But

The Euston Tap.

CARLISLE.
CARNARVON.
CHESTER.
CORK.
COVENTRY.
DERBY.
DEWSBURY.
DUDLEY.
DUBLIN.

DUMFRIES.
DUNDEE.
EDINBURGH.
FLEETWOOD.
GLASGOW.
GREENOCK.
HALIFAX.
HEREFORD.
HUDDERSFIELD

rail contractors need not have feared – soon railway systems (i.e., locomotives, track and stations) were being exported to the USA, Canada, Argentina and the British Empire.

The 12 termini produced a road traffic nightmare in London. Disgorging thousands of passengers on the periphery who then took to horse-drawn transport to complete their journey. A solution was needed to alleviate the grid lock at rush hour, and the most favoured plan was to go underground (see page 117).

Euston station, designed by Philip Hardwick, was a monumental edifice of Classical Greek architecture, intended to reassure customers of this safe and solid mode of transport. Sadly, and to great criticism, the entire station was demolished in the 1960s and replaced with today's functional, but architecturally unremarkable, slab of concrete. All that remains of the original station are two modest station buildings at the front (former ticket offices) adorned with destinations carved in stone. King's Cross, St. Pancras and Paddington are all now Grade I listed buildings.

The Euston Tap is housed in one of the former ticket offices. Possibly the smallest pub in this book, it still manages to squeeze in an American-style basement bar and an upstairs bar – combining to serve up an extensive line of draught beers, ciders and wines.

The Castle

34–35 Cowcross St, London EC1M 6DB

Going underground

'Take The Twopenny Tube And Avoid All Anxiety', so went the advertising slogan for the Central Line in 1900. And many millions heeded the advice, on what is now still the world's third largest underground network (after Shanghai and Beijing) – providing more than one billion passenger rides per annum.

The aptly named Metropolitan Line was the world's first underground railway. Built in 1863 it ferried passengers from the main line termini in west and north London (i.e., Paddington, Euston and King's Cross) to the central business district, the City at Farringdon. It used the 'cut and cover' technique so not requiring deep excavations but causing havoc on the surface. As did the District Line that connected Kensington to Westminster (i.e., the political centre) in 1868, subsequently connected to the Circle Line in 1874.

All lines used steam trains, causing huge discomfort from the sound and steam emissions – only alleviated by blowholes in pavements for tunnel ventilation. In 1890, the City and South London Railway (today the Northern Line) heralded two firsts. It was the world's first deep level line and used electric trains powered by direct current, initially pulling carriages with no windows. The Waterloo and City Line (1898) and Central Line (1900) followed using the same methods of construction and locomotion.

All lines were privately owned and operated, but without government financial support struggled to make a return. The situation was alleviated by the arrival of two American investors a few years apart: Charles Tyson Yerkes and Albert Stanley. Yerkes formed the Underground Electric Railways of London (UERL) in 1902, completed works with the latest American engineering, and employed Leslie Green to provide a corporate image (evident today in the use of red and green station tiling). Stanley (Lord Ashfield) joined UERL in 1907 – and later founded London Underground in 1933, with himself as Chairman and Frank Pick as Managing Director. The 1920s and 30s also saw Charles Holden and Harry Beck employed, respectively, as the station and tube map designers. The Victoria Line (1969) and Jubilee Line (1979) followed much later in the century. All tube trains were liveried in unpainted silver aluminium until 1985, when graffiti forced a periodic repainting programme.

The Castle pub was opened shortly after Farringdon Station was built, providing a drinking stop before heading for one of the mainline termini and home. Victorian design, good food and a wide range of drinks make an historical and welcoming atmosphere.

The Castle.

12

CULTURE

The Anchor

34 Park St, London SE1 9EF

Theatre is born

Shakespeare was born in Stratford-upon-Avon in 1564 and spent the greater part of his working life in London – living and working north of the Thames (Shoreditch) in the City of London (Blackfriars) and south of the Thames (Bankside).

Theatre in the City of London in the late 1500s was underground and rare since performances were banned owing to its bawdy reputation. Theatre could only be performed in places like Blackfriars, Shoreditch and over the river in Southwark – locations all outside the jurisdiction of the City.

At Blackfriars, in 1576, a venue was set up in the former Blackfriars Dominican priory. Whilst technically inside the City boundary, it had certain legal freedoms as a 'liberty'. At Blackfriars, the 'Children of the Chapel Royal' (an all-children company) played to a public comfortable in the knowledge that their performers were free of corruption, bawdiness or other vices.

Shakespeare arrived in London in the mid-1590s. Already known as a playwright, he struck up an association with father and son team, James and Richard Burbage. James had built two theatres outside the City in Shoreditch: 'The Theatre' and 'The Curtain'. In 1594, a playing company was formed under the patronage of Queen Elizabeth I: the 'Lord Chamberlain's Men' (named after the Queen's head of court entertainment). It commissioned Shakespeare to write plays, such as *Hamlet, Othello, King Lear*, and *Macbeth*, which were performed at The Theatre, with the 'Bard' performing secondary roles. All was good for a few years.

In 1596, The Theatre closed (due to a dispute with the freeholder) and the Burbages shipped the physical building to Bankside on the south side of the river in Southwark (outside restrictions placed on theatre in the City) – rebuilding and renaming it the Globe Theatre. Meanwhile, performances of the Lord Chamberlain's Men continued at the Curtain Theatre. The Globe opened for business in 1599 and remained in operation until 1642 when it closed for good – albeit with a year's gap in 1613 when it was damaged by pyrotechnics during a performance of *Henry VIII*. The original site of the 'The Globe' is well marked in Park Street, Southwark – about 200 metres from its modern-day representation.

In 1603, the company was re-named 'The King's Men' after King James I. The Globe was operating nicely during the summer months and in 1608, the Burbages sought a location on the north bank for winter performances. They took possession of the former Blackfriars Dominican priory (mentioned earlier). The Blackfriars Playhouse remained here until 1655, until it was shut down by Cromwell's puritanical government (see page 53). Blackfriars Playhouse stood in modern-day Playhouse Yard – *The Winter's Tale* and *Cymbeline* were written with the Blackfriars Playhouse in mind.

The Anchor pub is on the south side of the Thames, opposite Blackfriars and to the east of the Globe Theatre. Serving beer from 1616, as a 'tap room' for the adjacent brewery, it's a rare survivor of the river taverns popular in Shakespeare's time. A Greene King pub, it offers a good selection of drinks, an extensive range of classic pub food along with vegan, vegetarian and non-gluten options.

Traveller's tip: don't miss 'Shakespeare's Gatehouse' which is near Playhouse Yard. The gatehouse

The Anchor.

was next to the current day Cockpit pub and is the only property known to have been owned by Shakespeare in London.

The Chandos

29 St Martin's Lane, London WC2N 4DD

Britain embraces art

Despite Britain's relatively late entry into art appreciation, the National Gallery ranks among the world's top galleries – especially for the

French Impressionist collection and impressionist-style J.M.W. Turners, pre-dating the French school by some 30 years.

Entering the game late in 1824, Parliament agreed to pay £60,000 to the banker-art collector John Julius Angerstein for 38 of his paintings. This would form the core of the nation's art collection, to be accessible free by all. To the amusement of the French (since Britain had nothing to compare with The Louvre) the pictures were initially displayed at Angerstein's house in Pall Mall.

In 1831, plans were agreed for a National Gallery, designed by William Wilkins, to be situated on the north side of Trafalgar Square – the very centre of London. Opening in 1837, the gallery housed the founding collection and developed along the lines of tastes of the day: Correggio and Titian (Italian School), Rubens and Rembrandt (Dutch), Claude and Poussin (French) and Reynolds, Hogarth and Lawrence (British). Today, there are 2,300 works of art including van Eyck's *Arnolfini Portrait*, Velázquez's *Rokeby Venus*, Van Gogh's *Sunflowers* and Turner's *Fighting Temeraire*.

Pre-dating the National Gallery, the Royal Academy of Arts was Britain's first art school, founded in 1768. Its inaugural

The Chandos.

National Gallery.

National Gallery (entrance hall).

president was Sir Joshua Reynolds. Originally based in Somerset House on Aldwych, it was relocated to the National Gallery in 1837 and then its present home, Burlington House, Piccadilly in 1868. Today, the collection is the culmination of art works donated by former Academicians (by obligation) and gifts or purchases, consisting of works by Reynolds, Gainsborough, Constable, Turner and Michelangelo, plus frequent world-class Loan Exhibitions.

Trumping both the National Gallery and the Royal Academy is the Royal Collection – some of which can be viewed in London at the Queen's Gallery, adjacent to Buckingham Place. The bulk of the collection can be viewed at the king's properties throughout the UK. The collection is not owned personally by king but is held in trust by him as monarch for his successors and the nation. It is one of the largest and most important art collections in the world, and one of the last great European royal collections to remain intact. All this, despite its greater part being sold, by order of Oliver Cromwell, following the execution of King Charles I (see page 53). It includes works by Titian, Raphael, da Vinci, Bellini, Mantegna (*Triumphs of Caesar*, saved by Cromwell) and Vermeer.

The Chandos is directly opposite the National Gallery and is a large pub with snug cubicles and plenty of standing room. Being in the 'West End', and adjacent to the London Coliseum (home of the English National Opera), there are interesting displays of theatrical and operatic memorabilia. It's a Sam Smiths pub, so expect a good selection of ales and beers, plus foodie favourites.

Paxton's Head

153 Knightsbridge, London SW1X 7PA

Albertopolis

In 1850, Britain was at its peak of world dominance. The arrival of Germany, Japan and the USA as industrial powers was still 30 years away and Britain, along with its colonies and protectorates, had first right of refusal to supply the world's largest market: the British Empire.

Minds turned to brandishing the fruits of the empire with a giant display of its crafts and wares. A Royal Commission was formed, chaired by Prince Albert and comprising Prime Minister Russell, former and future PMs (Peel and Gladstone), Thomas Cubitt (see page 101), Charles Barry (see page 69) and the man whose idea it all was, Henry Cole.

Hyde Park was selected as the site for the exhibition and over 230 entries for the design of the building were submitted. Joseph Paxton's City of Birmingham produced the cast iron and glass edifice that was selected as the winning scheme. Measuring over 560m by 140m it took only eight months to construct. The Whig government of the day funded the venture, realising it could be made self-financing by charging a one shilling entry fee –

something that around six million people availed themselves of.

On 1 May 1851, Queen Victoria opened the Great Exhibition, welcoming an average of 40,000 visitors per day for over five months. It was an astounding public success, comprising nearly 100,000 exhibits from Britain and all over the world. Exhibits comprised items such as engines, carriages, textiles, china, glass, porcelain and all types of decorative arts. Britain displayed its most recent gift from India: the Koh-i-Noor diamond, now part of the Crown Jewels. The United States of America bucked the trend for

decorative arts and displayed the latest Colt revolver, a Goodyear rubber tyre and an unpickable lock – designs firmly rooted in industry.

The exhibition produced a vast surplus of £186,000, which was invested in a permanent centre for the display of science, arts and manufactures. Coined 'Albertopolis' at the time, it is evidenced today by

Right: *Royal Albert Hall.*

Below: *Paxton's Head.*

the museums strung out on Exhibition Road immediately to the south of the former site of Paxton's Crystal Palace. The site is remembered today by plaques and boundary markers along South Carriage Drive. The building was dismantled in 1852 and moved to a permanent home in Sydenham, sadly to be consumed by the ravages of fire in 1936.

Paxton's Head is located near the former site of the Great Exhibition, built in 1900, at the close of the Victorian period. Named after its architect, the Grade II listed pub is typical of the late Victorian architectural style – with oak panels, striking etched mirrors and original tiling. It's a Greene King pub offering an excellent range of cask ales and classic British dishes.

The Ship

116 Wardour St, London W1F 0TT

It's only Rock 'n' Roll

The foundations of Soho were discussed earlier (see page 96). Its reputation as a centre of rock and pop music can be traced to the Second World War when the genre was introduced by American troops stationed in London.

The arrival of Italians in Soho in the 1950s fused coffee culture with pop. The 2i's Coffee Bar in Old Compton Street (now Poppies fish and chip restaurant) was set up by brothers Freddie and Sammy Irani. Teens, attracted by the Gaggia coffee machine and an American jukebox, made it the place to open a small performance venue. And it is here that British Rock 'n' Roll music burst onto the scene – featuring stars like Cliff Richard and Tommy Steele.

An edgier form of rock music was born at the shop on the corner of Broadwick Street (off Wardour Street) and Duck Lane. Formerly the Bricklayer's Arms, it's where the Rolling Stones auditioned (Mick Jagger and Keith Richards both responding to an advertisement placed by Brian Jones in *Jazz Week*) and first rehearsed in an upstairs room between March and April

The Ship.

1962. Their first gig in July 1962 was just around the corner at the Marquee Club in Oxford Street. Moving to Wardour Street in 1964, the club was London's premier rock venue until 1988, hosting almost every major rock band.

With its reputation established as the beating heart of British rock music, Soho was chosen by the Sheffield Brothers for Trident Studios (1968–1981), competing with Abbey Road Studios in west London, famed venue for recording sessions by The Beatles. The latest 8-track technology attracted a host of artists to the modest building in St Anne's Court (off Wardour Street). The list of artists that recorded at Trident

Studies is prodigious: David Bowie, Lou Reed, Elton John, Queen, Carly Simon, Genesis, The Beatles (who switched to record *Hey Jude*) and many more displayed in the widow of the building.

Ronnie Scott established his modern jazz club in Chinatown in 1959, moving to Frith Street in Soho in 1965. Most of the greats have played here. Not only an outstanding saxophonist, but Ronnie was also a master of the one-liner; quipping remarks like, 'I love this place, reminds me of home: filthy and full of strangers'!

Soho's popularity fuelled a meteoric rise in property prices in the 60s – and made Paul Raymond a billionaire from

Chinatown.

Above: *Raymond Revuebar.*

Below: *Ronnie Scott's.*

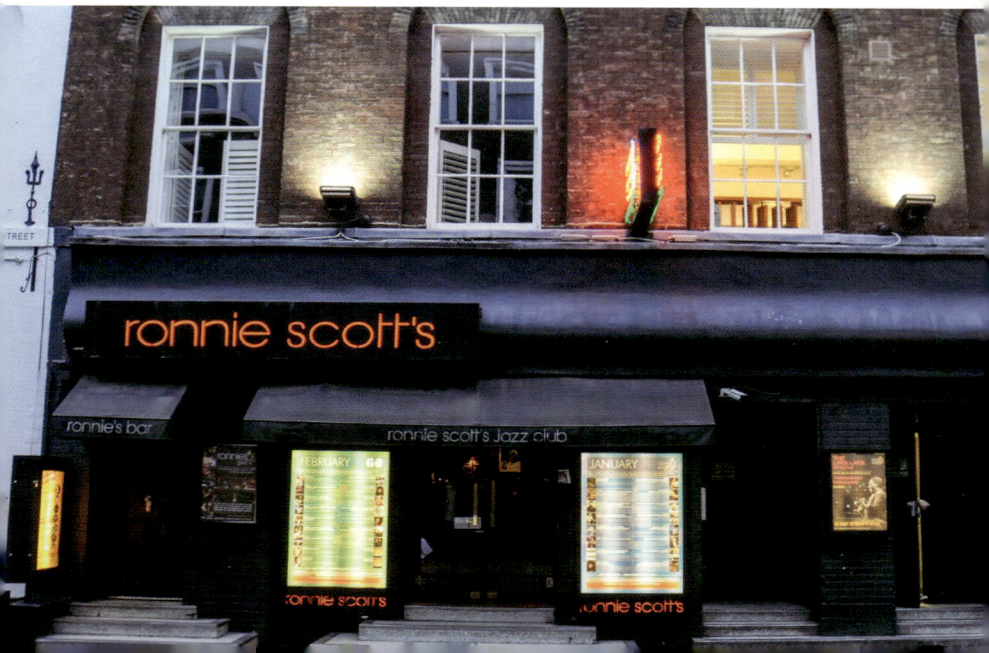

Soho Square.

his astute property investments and empire based in Soho. The Raymond Revuebar combined jazz and exotic dancers; a winning combination aided by his astute musical arranger Norman Moy.

With many of the venues now repurposed, it's a relief one can still visit The Ship pub on Wardour Street. It served as the after-show bar for The Marquee Club, when the club first opened without an alcohol licence. It continues to serve as the Marquee's local, and photographs on the walls recall the heydays of the 1960s. Billing itself as the pub that starts rocking when the sun goes down, this Fullers establishment has the heritage to support the claim!

13

REFORM

Ye Olde Cheshire Cheese

145 Fleet St, London EC4A 2BP

Read all about it

The appropriately named Wynkyn de Worde set up a publishing and printing business in Fleet Street in around 1500 – after leaving the employ of William Caxton (who first introduced the printing press to England at Westminster in around 1475).

Fleet Street rapidly became the centre of book publishing, printing, binding and retailing and later journalism – right up to 1986 when the exodus of newspaper publishing to new presses and premises in the east heralded the end of Fleet Street as a centre of publishing.

London's first newspaper, *The Daily Courant*, was published on 11 March 1702. A single page broadsheet, it concentrated on foreign news, gossip and advertisements. The modern day *The Spectator* can trace it roots to these early beginnings. *The Daily Post* and *The Daily Chronicle* followed, serving up a similar diet to the *Courant*. It wasn't until the easing of reporting restrictions on government that serious journalism started with publication of *The London Times* in 1785. All these papers were published on or near Fleet Street. (NB: *The London Gazette* pre-dated the other titles, coming into being in 1666 under authority of Charles I, but was more of a court circular and not for sale to the public).

A statue in Fetter Lance, off Fleet Street, commemorates the publisher, MP and City of London Lord Mayor, John Wilkes. In 1771, after years of campaigning, arrest and charges of sedition, Wilkes was able use his influence in the City to force the government to allow the reporting of debates – thereby opening up the freedom of the press. Later in the eighteenth and nineteenth centuries Fleet Street was the location of head offices of the *Daily Telegraph*, *Daily Express* and *Daily Mail* – until all followed the lead of *The Times* and moved east to new premises and modern technology. Journalism was assisted by Dr Samuel Johnson, who published his *Dictionary of the English Language* in 1775, after years of compilation from his home nestled

Ye Old Cheshire Cheese

Hot & Cold
Bar Food

Restaurants
Open Daily For
Lunch & Dinner

Private Parties
Catered For

Famous Through
Four Centuries
Ye Old Cheshire
Cheese
Rebuilt in 1667
Known Haunt Of

Charles Dickens &
Countless Others

**Ye Olde
Cheshire Cheese
Rebuilt 1667**
in the reign of Charles II
and successively
in the reigns of

James II	1685–1688
Interregnum Dec 11 1688–Feb 13 1689	
William III & Mary II	1689–1702
Anne	1702–1714
George I	1714–1727
George II	1727–1760
George III	1760–1820
George IV	1820–1830
William I	1830–1837
Victoria	1837–1901
Edward VII	1901–1910
George V	1910–1936
Edward VIII	1936
George VI	1936–1952
Elizabeth II	1952

Ye Olde Cheshire Cheese.

Dr Johnson's House.

Statue of Dr Samuel Johnson, St Clement Danes Church.

in Gough Square (off Fleet Street) – a hidden gem that can be visited today. At the west of Fleet Street, Hoare & Co. is London's oldest privately owned bank. Founded in 1672, it recently saw off its neighbour, Childs Bank (established earlier in 1664 but closed in 2022).

Ye Olde Cheshire Cheese states outside that it was rebuilt in 1667, after the Great Fire, although research shows there has been a tavern on the site since the 1530s. The Chop Room with its private booth-style seating arrangement was a favourite of Dr Johnson and others. From the basement to three floors up, snugs, fires and sawdust-covered floors exude the atmosphere of early London. Charles Dickens frequented the main bar, as did Thomas Carlyle and Lord Alfred Tennyson – along with a host of other writers and painters to the modern-day. A drink here is one of London's most authentic pub experiences.

Morpeth Arms

58 Millbank, London SW1P 4RW

Watching the wheels go round

Long term confinement of convicted criminals is a relatively new practice – only becoming a punishment in 1840. Prior to that felons were either executed (see pages 78, 81) or transported to British overseas colonies (introduced in 1718). The exceptions were debtors who were held in special debtors prisons (named compters) until their debts were paid – one can visit the remaining walls of the Marshalsea Prison for debtors in Southwark.

The loss of the American colonies in 1782 (the main destination for transportation) presented an acute crisis in prisoner capacity. A solution was found by housing prisoners in decommissioned ships moored on the Thames at Woolwich (called prison hulks), prisoners often undertaking hard labour on the docks and dredging the river. The recognition that execution was too harsh a punishment for many crimes added to the capacity problem and on many occasions during the 1700s, Parliament would pass acts to discharge prisoners to free-up space.

In 1777, shocked at the conditions under which prisoners were held, John Howard (a high sheriff) campaigned for better organisation of prisons, with individual cells and separate sections for the sexes, young and old – plus the abolition of jail fees that were preventing prisoners from being released! Shortly after, the 1779 Penitentiary Act was passed by Parliament. But due to pressures of conflict in Europe, not least the Napoleonic Wars, it would be nearly 40 years before the first of these new style prisons was built at Millbank in Westminster. Providing some respite in 1789, Britain resumed transportation to the new colony of Australia – a policy that lasted until 1869. The Howard League is still the modern-day penal reform charity.

Quakers, such as Elizabeth Fry, were instrumental in driving the reform of prisons – supported later by the popular works of Charles Dickens (e.g., *David Copperfield* and *Little Dorrit*), whose own father John had been imprisoned in Marshalsea Prison when he was 10 years old.

The Millbank Penitentiary opened in 1816 with two further innovations: the American-inspired separates system of confinement and the treadmill or hand crank for hard labour sentences – subsequently adopted by many prisons across the UK including Pentonville in north London in 1842. National uniformity of conditions was achieved by the Prison Act of 1877. In part due to the land value, Millbank was closed in 1890 to make way for the Tate Britain art gallery. Today, the penal system continues to evolve, adopting ever more progressive policies of education, training and assimilation preparing for post-prison life.

Morpeth Arms.

The Morpeth Arms is located on the site of the former Millbank Penitentiary. Aside from a fine bar stocking craft beers and drinks, seasonally curated menus and views of the river it boasts the original holding cells used before prisoners were shipped down-under – and which can be visited by prior arrangement.

Sherlock Holmes

10 Northumberland St, London WC2N 5DB

Policing the capital

On 29 September 1829 the Home Secretary's 'boys in blue' first stepped out onto the streets of London to walk their 'beats'. Surprisingly, the so-called 'bobbies' (after Secretary Robert Peel) weren't fully welcomed by the public. In this febrile period of European conflict and rebellion, any state intervention on liberty was regarded with suspicion. Blue was chosen for the uniform and a top hat to distance it from any military similarities – along with a wooden truncheon and a rattle for raising the alarm.

The Metropolitan Police Force was headquartered at 4 Whitehall Place near Great Scotland Yard in Westminster, so named since the area was formerly the London home of

Scottish monarchy before the Union in 1707. Shortened to 'Scotland Yard', the HQ moved to Victoria Embankment (i.e., Norman Shaw building) in 1890, then to 10 Broadway in 1967 before returning to Victoria Embankment in 2016. Since moving in 1890, the headquarters have been known as 'New Scotland Yard'.

Prior to the 'Met', arrangements for policing the capital were rudimentary. In 1749, after years of frustration of dealing with theft and violence with only a volunteer force of elderly 'Charlies' at his disposal Henry Fielding, the famous author and magistrate, and his blind brother John established the professional 'Bow Street Runners'. John became the driving force after Henry became seriously unwell soon after the force's creation. Growing to a force of only 68 runners by 1800, it wasn't entirely effective at policing nearly one million people! Fortunately, river-based crime (significant owing to tonnes of goods being held on the river awaiting unloading), was the remit of the Thames Police (later the River Police), established in 1798. The Bow Street Runners and the Thames Police were merged with the 'Met' in 1839.

The Metropolitan Police covered wider London but had no jurisdiction

Sherlock Holmes.

within the City of London. The City had the right to govern its own affairs since time immemorial (see page 56). Here, policing evolved through obligatory service by citizens to a professional merchant-funded day and night watch system numbering 1,000 'watchmen' and managed by the City's local government (the Common Council).

Following the creation of the Metropolitan Police, proposals were put to Parliament to merge the City's police with the 'Met'. Strongly opposed to it, the City countered with a proposal to create its own City of London police force. This was passed and it was established on 17 August 1839. London still has two police forces – the City of London Police and the Metropolitan Police.

The Victorian-period Sherlock Holmes pub and beer garden is a fitting location to contemplate the consultations between Inspector Lestrade of Scotland Yard and Holmes. It is located close to Great Scotland Yard. Its interior is packed with Holmes memorabilia and references to the many books of his creator Sir Arthur Conan Doyle. Upstairs there is a fine recreation of Holmes' famous Baker Street flat, including rare artefacts. A good range of real ales, wines, other drinks and quality British food will soon have you reeling off passages from the books. Elementary!

Traveller's tip: the original stables for some of the horses of the Mounted Branch is still operational at 7 Great Scotland Yard.

The White Bear

138 Kennington Park Rd, London SE11 4DJ

Political reform
In 1780, only 3 per cent of the adult population were entitled to vote. Worse still, all the new large industrial cities

The White Bear.

of the north (Leeds, Manchester etc.) did not have a single MP between them. Yet in land-owning areas (later called 'rotten boroughs') one or two MPs represented tiny populations.

The Great Reform Act of 1832, under the government of Charles Grey, extended the electorate to males over 21, abolished rotten boroughs and extended the franchise to 67 new cities and towns – but entitlement to vote still maintained a property qualification equivalent to £10 rent pa.

Owing to dissatisfaction with the 1832 Act, a People's Charter was drawn up by the London Working Men's

Association in 1838. The so called 'Chartists' had six demands: all men should have the vote, ballots should be secret and annual, constituencies should be of equal size, MPs should be paid and the property qualification for becoming an MP should be abolished. The major rally of April 1848 took place on Kennington Common and was attended by more than 25,000 people – causing great government concern of riots. Heavily policed it was, in the end, peaceful, but resulted in the Common subsequently being enclosed by the government and the cricket fields relocated to a nearby market garden (renamed the Oval Cricket Club!).

A second reform act was passed in 1867 under the government of Benjamin Disraeli. It enfranchised all males over 21 regardless of a property qualification, but stipulated they must be skilled and settled. William Gladstone's government passed a third reform act in 1884 that also gave the vote to unskilled men.

The original Chartists were eventually successful in most of their demands – but not until 1918, when having been relied on so heavily in the war effort, women over 30 were also enfranchised. And by 1928 there was universal suffrage for men and women at 21 – with no property restrictions on women.

During this hundred years of reform, some laws were progressive – like the repeal of the Corn Laws in 1846 (a protection regime that set an artificially high price on wheat to protect land owners from American competition). And others regressive, such as the Poor Law of 1834 reverting responsibility for the care of the poor from parishes to government-funded 'poor law unions' – where the poor were housed, clothed, fed and worked for several hours each day in purpose-built workhouses.

Concerned with invasion by the French (or rebellion by the Jacobites) Catholics were denied equivalence until the Catholic Relief Act of 1778 made some amends in the areas of property ownership, inheritance and joining the Army – the latter sparking the 1780 Gordon Riots throughout London. A second relief act in 1780 permitted Catholic schools and bishops. But it would take until 1829 (following defeat of the French in the Napoleonic Wars, 1793–1815) to pass legislation that permitted Catholics to become MPs, pushed through Parliament by the Duke of Wellington (PM) – partly to avert civil war in Ireland, which had joined the UK in 1801.

The White Bear pub near Kennington Common has been on this site since 1780. Witness to political reforms and a popular local for the Oval Cricket Ground, it serves a good selection of ales, wine and hot beverages, and specialises in Sunday roasts.

14

DIVERSITY

The Truman Brewery

91 Brick Lane, London E1 6QR

With open arms

London is the most prototypical city of immigrants in the world. Leaving aside the ancient and medieval conquest of the country by the Celts, Romans, Saxons, Vikings and Normans, London has welcomed diverse races, colours and creeds from the world over.

Under the Normans, Jews came to live in England, but later suffered persecution and were forced to leave in 1290 (until Oliver Cromwell revoked that in the 1650s). Industry and trade attracted craftsmen (particularly weavers), brewers and foreign merchants from the low countries and Germany – a trend that accelerated in the late 1500s as protestants fled religious persecution.

Spitalfields is an historic area to the east of the City of London. Since the 1660s, it has been the traditional first stop for immigrants arriving in London – and has suffered its share of poverty and destitution. Today, the area is a melting pot of the creative industries, street art and bohemian residents. Many of the original foundations are still there, represented by its people, cultures and architecture, making Spitalfields one of the most vibrant areas of London.

Among the first immigrant communities to arrive in Spitalfields were French Protestants, forced to flee France when the government made Protestantism unlawful (by revoking the 'Edict of Nantes'). The French brought their skills in silk weaving to England and both Spitalfields and Wandsworth were centres for these industries. In Spitalfields, the wealth created by silk industries has resulted in the largest remaining concentration of Georgian buildings in London – ironically saved by the subsequent economic decline of the area right up to the 1980s.

Jewish immigrants arrived in the 1880s, escaping anti-Semitism and violence in Eastern Europe. Silk weaving started to give way to clothing and brewing as the principal industries around Spitalfields – evidenced today by the continuing 'rag trade' and former breweries. In more recent times, Spitalfields has become home to the

Bangladeshi community, introducing a prosperous wholesale clothing economy – along with the best curry houses in London. Brick Lane Mosque is a fascinating reminder of the richness of immigrant communities in this part of London. Built in 1743 by French Protestants (Huguenots), it became a Methodist chapel, a synagogue, and since 1976, a mosque.

The potato famine in the 1840s was a catalyst for immigrants from Ireland. Their story has been one of frequent hardship as they toiled with the hardest work (e.g., canal and railway building).

After the Second World War, the British Nationality Act 1948 encouraged immigration from Commonwealth countries by offering full British citizenship – largely to rebuild the country owing to severe labour shortages. Many Jamaicans first arrived in Clapham and Brixton (being temporarily housed in underground shelters), areas that retain a strong black cultural heritage. In the 1960s many immigrants came from India and Pakistan and as refugees from Uganda. As key wartime allies, London also became a favoured destination for Poles when Poland joined the EU in 2004 – coming to an end after Britain left Europe in 2020.

The Truman Brewery, formerly the Black Eagle Brewhouse, has a history

Truman Brewery.

Vintage Market, Brick Lane.

Bagel Shop, Brick Lane.

Street art, Brick Lane.

stretching back to the 1660s – and brewing itself to the Dutch who introduced hops to England in the late 1200s. The brewery closed in 1988, and the site is now an exciting arts quarter, hosting shops, galleries, markets, bars and restaurants centred around Brick Lane.

Did you know? Chinese sailors started arriving in London from 1800, settling in Limehouse – before moving to Soho following devastation in the Second World War. Each year, hundreds of thousands descend on the West End to enjoy a colourful parade, free stage performances and fireworks – the largest Chinese New Year celebrations outside of Asia.

Royal Vauxhall Tavern

372 Kennington Lane, London SE11 5HY

Gay's the word

Sex between males in England and its dominions was first outlawed by an Act of Parliament in 1533. Punishable by death, it was eventually repealed to a minimum of 10 years imprisonment in 1861. Acts in private were also outlawed in the Criminal Law Amendment Act 1885 – the act that Oscar Wilde fell victim to. Throughout this long period, female homosexuality was never viewed as attracting much interest and therefore legislation never passed against it.

After the Second World War there was a rise in arrests and prosecutions of homosexual men – many of whom held significant posts and achievements, such as Alan Turing the renowned cryptographer. The number of arrests called into question the laws. The Wolfenden Report (1957) prioritised public protection over scrutinising people's private lives and recommended that homosexual behaviour between consenting adults in private should be no

Royal Vauxhall Tavern.

longer a criminal offence. Legislation allowing sex between men over 21 was eventually decriminalised by the 1967 Sexual Offences Act. From that date, things gradually improved; 1972 seeing London's first Pride and the Liberal Democrats becoming the first UK political party to support equality in 1975.

But in the 1980s, HIV and AIDS struck Britain. This hardened attitudes to gay sex, seemingly justifying by the Local Government Act of 1988 that outlawed the promotion and publishing of homosexual material in maintained schools – the so-called Section 28. Section 28 was repealed in 2003, the same year that UK courts were empowered to give tougher sentences for offences motivated by a victim's sexual orientation (Section 146 of the Criminal Justice Act). Age restrictions were then decreased to 18 (in 1994) and 16 (in 2001). Slow and painful progress. Today, gay people can marry after legislation was passed in various marriage acts in England, Scotland and Northern Ireland (between 2013 and 2020).

Throughout much of this period the redoubtable Royal Vauxhall Tavern (RVT) has been a sanctuary and performance venue for many gay people, even since its foundation in the 1863 – the pub being built on the site of the Georgian Vauxhall Pleasure Gardens (closed in 1859), renowned for fashion and sexual liberation and perhaps setting a precedent for the RVT in later years.

The RVT is the UK's first building to be awarded Grade II listed status for its contribution to LGBTQ+ history. Specialising in drag performances, it's hosted stars such as the late Dame Edna and Lily Savage. Such is its influence, that Paul O'Grady referred to it as 'the Royal Vauxhall Tavern School of Dramatic Art'. Not make-believe, the venue won the award for the Best LGBTQ+ Cabaret Venue at the 2020 Media and Entertainment Industry Awards. There are other gay pubs, particularly in Soho but the RVT is the first and foremost.

(Gay's the Word is London's most famous LGBTQ+ bookshop in Bloomsbury.)

FURTHER READING

Ackroyd, Peter. *Dominion: the history of England from the Battle of Waterloo to Victoria's Diamond Jubilee.* (New York: St. Martin's Press, 2018).

Cannadine, David. *Victorious Century: The United Kingdom, 1800-1906.* (London: Penguin, 2018, first pub. 2017).

Cannon, John and Crowcraft, Robert. *The Oxford Companion to British History.* (OUP, 2015, first pub. 1997).

Darwin, John. *The empire project: the rise and fall of the British world-system, 1830-1970.* (Cambridge: CUP, 2009).

Ferguson, Niall. *Empire, how Britain made the modern world.* (London: Penguin Books, 2003).

Hayden, P. and Hampson, T. *London's best pubs.* (London: New Holland, 2011).

Hobsbawm, Eric. J. *Volume 3, the Penguin economic history of Britain: industry and empire.* (London: Penguin, 1990, first pub. 1968).

Jenkins, S. *A short history of England.* (London: Profile Books, 2018, first pub. 2011).

Kynaston, David. *City of London: The History.* (London: Vintage, 2011, first published 1994).

Marr, Andrew. *The making of modern Britain.* (London: Macmillan, 2009).

Porter, S. *The story of London* (Stroud: Amberley, 2016).

Weinreb, B., Hibbert, C. et.al. *The London Encyclopaedia* (London: Macmillan, 2008, first pub. 1983).

Wilson, A.N. *London, a short history.* (London: Phoenix, 2004).

Winks, Robin. *The Oxford history of the British Empire, Volume 5.* (Oxford: OUP, 1999).

INDEX